2005–2006 Annual Supplement to

THE PIANO BOOK

BUYING & OWNING A NEW OR USED PIANO

LARRY FINE

BROOKSIDE PRESS • BOSTON, MASSACHUSETTS

Brookside Press
P.O. Box 178, Jamaica Plain, Massachusetts 02130
(617) 522-7182
(800) 888-4741 (orders: Independent Publishers Group)

info@pianobook.com
www.pianobook.com

Printed in the United States of America

Distributed to the book trade by Independent Publishers Group,
814 North Franklin St., Chicago, IL 60610
(800) 888-4741 or (312) 337-0747

ISBN 1-929145-17-9 (print edition)
ISBN 1-929145-18-7 (electronic edition)

NOTICE

Reasonable efforts have been made to secure accurate information for this publication. Due in part to the fact that manufacturers and distributors will not always willingly make this information available, however, some indirect sources have been relied upon.

Neither the author nor publisher make any guarantees with respect to the accuracy of the information contained herein and will not be liable for damages—incidental, consequential, or otherwise—resulting from the use of the information.

INTRODUCTION

Given the long time span between new editions of *The Piano Book*, it's impractical to provide in the book itself the detailed model and price data that piano shoppers increasingly seek. Similarly, updated information about manufacturers and products is needed in a timely manner. This *Annual Supplement to The Piano Book*, published each summer, is designed to fill that information gap. I hope this modest companion volume will effectively extend the "shelf life" of *The Piano Book* as a valuable reference work, and serve as an additional information resource for piano buyers and piano lovers.

Larry Fine

June, 2005

CONTENTS

MANUFACTURER and PRODUCT UPDATE

This section describes changes to companies, products, and brand names since the fourth edition of *The Piano Book* went to press in the fall of 2000. This section is cumulative; that is, information contained in last year's *Supplement*, to the extent it is still accurate, is repeated here and changes that have occurred during the past year have been added. If a company or brand name is not listed here, it means that there is nothing new of substance to report.

It is not intended, of course, that the information in this update section take the place of the reviews in *The Piano Book*. With some exceptions, the update is limited to changes of a factual nature only, whereas the main book contains, in addition, critical reviews, ratings, and recommendations. Readers should understand that, in most cases, changes in the quality of any particular brand of piano occur very slowly, over a period of many years, if at all. Only where there has been an abrupt change in company ownership, or a period of rapid technological or economic change in the country of origin, is there likely to be a change in quality worth worrying about. For that reason, the reviews in *The Piano Book* can still be considered reliable unless otherwise noted here.

Trends

Pianos made in China continue to improve and make inroads into the North American market. By some estimates, more than one-quarter of all pianos sold in the U.S. in 2004 were made in China. As recently as 2001, most pianos from China, though technically acceptable, were not musically desirable. Over the past couple of years, however, the musical qualities have taken a big leap forward. Though nearly all makes have improved, and most are acceptable, the best vertical pianos are those from the Yantai-Perzina factory, sold here under the Carl Ebel, Perzina, and Gerh. Steinberg labels; the best grands are from the Dongbei factory, sold under the names Nordiska, Everett, Hallet & Davis, and Story & Clark, among others. Pearl River and Ritmüller pianos are also among the better ones. Palatino verticals, brand new last year, also look promising. The jury is still out as to whether these pianos will hold up over the long term and in demanding climates and situations. Anecdotal reports suggest less consistency than with pianos from other countries, but otherwise few major problems. Prices are so low, however, that for many entry-level buyers these pianos are an excellent value despite some uncertainty about their longevity. At least as short-term investments, and in milder climates and less demanding situations, they are probably fine.

(*The Piano Book* contains brand ratings organized by "group," each group representing a level of quality. At the time of publication, I placed most Chinese pianos in Group 5, the lowest level. At the present time, I would probably place most in Group 4, "Medium quality consumer-grade pianos." Although some actually exhibit the performance characteristics of higher grade instruments, due to their short track record caution would dictate describing them as Group 4 instruments for the time being. See *The Piano Book* for details.)

Although there has been an explosion of different brand names under which Chinese-made pianos are being marketed, there are only about eight Chinese manufacturers that make pianos for export to the U.S. Piano shoppers should keep in mind that, cosmetics aside, if two brands of piano originate in the same factory, they are probably very similar, if not identical.

On the other end of the price spectrum, European piano makers seem to be in a race to redesign their pianos for better sound projection and sustain, à la Steinway. While the European piano market is languishing, the U.S. market for high-end pianos, relatively speaking, is thriving, and for a number of companies, Steinway is the principal competitor. Considering how tradition-bound these companies are, this degree of activity is unusual. Some of the redesigns—new models from Seiler and Schimmel come to mind—have been terrific musical successes. My only worry is that the palette of available piano tonal qualities is becoming smaller and more homogeneous as the old-world sounds pass away.

Changes in China and in Europe, and their far-reaching consequences, are causing a paradigm shift in the piano industry that is making it more difficult to give advice to piano shoppers. A paradigm is a theoretical framework from which generalizations are formulated. For many years, the paradigm for piano quality has been an international pecking order with pianos from Russia and China (and, more recently, Indonesia) at the bottom, followed by Korea, Japan, Eastern Europe, and finally Western Europe (mostly Germany) at the top, with pianos from the United States scattered here and there depending on the brand. While this pecking order has never been foolproof, it has served its purpose as a generalization well enough for use by a generation of piano buyers.

Now these distinctions are being blurred by globalization. Unable to escape the high cost of doing business at home, some Western European manufacturers are developing satellite operations and more affordable second product lines in Eastern Europe. Some makers of high-end instruments are also quietly beginning to source parts and subassemblies from Asia and elsewhere. To the extent they can afford it, they are also investing in high-tech equipment to reduce the expense and inconsistency of hand labor, even while continuing to tout their status as makers of "hand-made" instruments. Some Korean and Chinese manufacturers, on the other hand, are importing parts and technology from Germany and Japan, producing instruments that when well prepared by the dealer rival the performance qualities of far more expensive pianos from Japan and, occasionally, Europe. The most we can say is that their longevity is unknown, an argument that, while true, becomes weaker with each passing year. In addition, global alliances such as that between Samick and Bechstein (described elsewhere in this *Supplement*) are sure to bring new products to the market that are more hybridized than anything we've seen before. Although the old paradigm still has validity, the number of nonconforming situations is increasing, all of which will cause temporary confusion in the marketplace until such time as a new paradigm emerges.

At the same time that quality differences between low-end and high-end instruments are becoming narrower, price difference are greater than they've ever been, bringing issues of "value" into greater prominence. Eastern European quality in some cases now closely approaches that of Western Europe, but at a price comparable to that of Japan. Some of the better pianos from China and Korea have specifications equal to almost anything from Japan, and workmanship nearly as good, at a fraction of the price. Caught in the middle, the Japanese are gradually being squeezed out of the piano market despite their perennially good quality.

Another consequence of globalization has been the diminishing number of suppliers of parts and materials (actions, hammers, pinblocks, soundboards, keys, plates, etc.) to the piano industry. (Actually, the enormous Chinese piano industry has numerous parts suppliers, but most of these supply parts only for pianos sold in the domestic Chinese market, not internationally.) At one time there were large differences in quality between suppliers, but globalization has reduced and sometimes eliminated those differences. For example, as recently as a few years ago, Detoa (Czech) actions were markedly inferior to Renner actions, and Chinese-made actions were terrible. Now there is at most only a small difference in quality between Detoa and Renner, virtually all Chinese actions are acceptable, and at least one Chinese supplier is said to be on the verge of producing credible knockoffs of Renner actions.

At the same time, many manufacturers continue to use a "recipe" approach to differentiating differently-priced piano lines: Choose an action (Renner, Detoa, Chinese), combine it with a hammer (Renner, Abel, Tokiwa), add a pinblock (Delignit, Dehonit, Bolduc), and so forth, to produce a piano at a particular price. But with fewer suppliers to choose from, and less difference between them, the implied difference in quality at different price points is threatening to become more a matter of image than actuality. Image has always been important in differentiating one piano brand from another, in part because even real differences can be subtle or highly technical and not obvious, especially to those who don't play the instrument well. But with even real differences evaporating, image-spinning is reaching new heights.

The above notwithstanding, differences still do exist. The most important is that between consumer-grade pianos on the one hand (Groups 3, 4, and 5) and performance-grade pianos on the other (Groups 1 and 2). There have been some attempts by makers to bridge this gap (i.e. Knabe by Samick and Kawai's Shigeru Kawai), but for the most part, the two different types of manufacturers still live in two different worlds. The difference between the two worlds is a bit less than it used to be, but it still exists in the form of selection, drying, and use of wood; final regulation and voicing; and attention to technical and cosmetic detail; in other words, the difference is more than just the "recipe." Theoretically, it would be possible for, say, a Chinese company to duplicate the finest pianos. But the market for these instruments is small, and some have unique and idiosyncratic designs that are not amenable to mass production. Therefore, it is always likely to be more of a niche market entered into by those whose profit-seeking is mixed with a love for the instrument and perhaps a desire to carry on a family business. At this point in time, such businesses are more likely to be Western than Asian, but who knows . . . that may one day change.

ALTENBURG

Correction to web site address: www.altenburgpiano.com

The F.E. Altenburg line of pianos made by Niendorf has been discontinued. The Beijing Piano Co. is making a new line of Altenburg pianos, some of which are special designs for Altenburg, with individually-hitched strings. Models up to 5' 3" use a laminated soundboard, larger models use solid spruce.

ASTIN-WEIGHT

Change to web site address: www.astin-weight.com

New e-mail address: gr8pianos@networld.com

Production of the 41" console has been temporarily suspended.

BALDWIN
including D.H. Baldwin, Hamilton, Chickering, Wurlitzer, Ellington, ConcertMaster

New address, phone, and ownership:

Baldwin Piano Company
309 Plus Park Blvd.
Nashville, Tennessee 37217

615-871-4500
800-876-2976

Owned by: Baldwin Piano, Inc., a wholly owned subsidiary of Gibson Guitar Corp.

Shortly after the fourth edition of *The Piano Book* was published in early 2001, the Baldwin board of directors hired a new management team to try to stave off impending bankruptcy caused by a series of costly mistakes and prior poor management. Avoiding bankruptcy turned out not to be possible, and the company filed for protection under Chapter 11 of the U.S. bankruptcy laws in May of 2001. On October 16, 2001, Baldwin's major creditor, General Electric Capital, purchased the company's assets at a court-ordered liquidation sale and then sold them to the Gibson Guitar Corp. on November 9, 2001.

Gibson owners Henry Juszkiewicz and Dave Berryman purchased Gibson in 1986 when it was in complete disarray and turned it into an extremely profitable and well-respected company. They feel that there are many parallels between Gibson's situation at that time and Baldwin's present situation, and expect to be able to turn Baldwin around as well.

Baldwin's new owners say they have made large capital investments to improve product quality. In order to make production more efficient, grand production has been moved from Conway, Arkansas and consolidated with vertical production in the company's Trumann, Arkansas facility. A woodworking plant in Greenwood, Mississippi closed in mid-2000 has had its functions transferred to a new woodworking plant in Trumann. The Juarez, Mexico action-making facility has been closed and its equipment divided between Baldwin plants in the U.S. and China. Additional cost savings have been realized by the transfer of all Baldwin sales, marketing, and administrative functions to Gibson headquarters in Nashville.

In 2004, Baldwin formed a joint venture with a piano manufacturer in Zhongshan, China, to be called Baldwin Zhongshan China, to produce pianos for the Chinese domestic market. In time, this factory is also expected to produce pianos and parts for Wurlitzer and other Baldwin-owned piano brands sold in the United States.

Prior to the management reorganization and subsequent bankruptcy, Baldwin had announced a number of changes to its product line, some of which were reported in *The Piano Book*. These changes were never fully realized due to the bankruptcy. The new owners plan to complete implementation of some of these changes (see comments below), and other changes are to be expected as Baldwin's reorganization evolves.

Baldwin's line of digital pianos has been discontinued.

The Eurostyle consoles and studios (E100, E101, E102, E250, E260) have been discontinued.

In the grands, the new model 225E is the model M (5' 2") in French Provincial styling. Model 226E is the model R (5' 8") in French Provincial styling. Model 227E is the model R with round, fluted, tapered legs, available only by special order. The 7' model SF-10 has been renamed SF-10E in honor of its adoption of the enhanced features of the upgraded Artist series grands (see *The Piano Book* for details).

The Chickering grands reported on in *The Piano Book* have been withdrawn. They were to be replaced by three new models—5' 4", 5' 9", and 6' 2"—made by Samick in Korea, with some cosmetic features taken from old Chickering designs. Due to Baldwin's bankruptcy, however, Baldwin never took possession of these pianos, so they were sold and warranted by Samick under license from Baldwin while supplies lasted. Baldwin still retains ownership of the Chickering trademark and may use it again in the future.

Also in the grand department, Baldwin has introduced a Custom Grand Finishes program, allowing customers to design their own grand piano. Four levels of customization are available: 1) wood-finish accents on regular grands; 2) colors (Jubilee Red, Golden Honey, Evergreen, Beale Street Blue, Madeira); 3) exotic wood veneers; and 4) anything you want. A Custom Vertical program includes the limited edition Gibson studio, each one signed by guitarist Les Paul, and the Elvis Presley Signature model, authorized by the Presley estate.

Baldwin has developed a new "Stealth"™ action, now used in all Baldwin vertical pianos. The "Full Blow" action, in use since 1939, has been updated with a Schwander-style hammer-butt return spring and other changes for improved quietness, responsiveness, durability, and ease of servicing. You can recognize the Stealth™ action by its visually striking black and deep blue colors. In addition, vertical pianos with the new action have model numbers ending in "E."

Baldwin has introduced several new lower-cost lines of piano. Only briefly introduced in 2003 and then discontinued was the Ellington brand name. This is a name originally produced by Baldwin from 1893 to 1930 as its lower-priced alternative to the Baldwin line. The most recent Ellingtons were made in China, verticals by the Beijing Piano Co. (see "Beijing") and grands by Sejung (see "Sejung").

The Ellington line has been replaced by the "Hamilton." Not to be confused with the famous Hamilton model studio piano Baldwin has made for decades with "Baldwin" on the fallboard, these new Hamiltons say "Hamilton" on the fallboard. Currently they are made in China by Sejung to Baldwin's specifications. The verticals are available in both continental and American furniture styles, have a solid spruce soundboard, and come with a ten-year parts and labor warranty. A 73-note spinet is part of this line. The company says that except for the number of notes, this short-keyboard instrument is a true acoustic piano with all the features of a full-size piano. The grands feature solid spruce soundboards and a ten-year parts and labor warranty.

Another new line is the D.H. Baldwin. Those in the piano trade may recall this as a name Baldwin used on a line of pianos made in Korea. The new D.H. Baldwin line, however, is made in Arkansas and is based on the Baldwin Acrosonic scale. The company says these new models are essentially like their higher-priced cousins musically, but with scaled-down cabinetry. Also made in Arkansas are pianos with a variety of minor brand names Baldwin owns and uses at dealer request, such as Ivers & Pond, Cable, J & C Fischer, and others. These are essentially the same as the D.H. Baldwin pianos.

As for Baldwin's Wurlitzer line of pianos, they are no longer made by Samick in Korea. Depending on demand, plant capacity, and other factors, parts may be made by Baldwin in China or the U.S., or by Sejung.

When Gibson acquired Baldwin, it acquired only its assets, not its liabilities. Therefore, the company is not required to honor warranty claims for pianos purchased prior to the acquisition date. Pianos purchased by the consumer from an authorized dealer on or after November 9, 2001 are eligible for warranty coverage, even if the dealer purchased the piano before that date. Warranty coverage for pianos purchased by the consumer before November 9, 2001 will only be considered on a case-by-case basis.

In mid-April 2002, Baldwin cancelled agreements with most of its dealers, retaining only the most active ones. Since then the company has been steadily rebuilding its dealer network, inviting new dealers to demonstrate their commitment, in part by making large purchases from the company. Baldwin says, however, that it *will* honor the warranty on pianos purchased from "cancelled" dealers, even though, technically, they are no longer "authorized" dealers.

BECHSTEIN, C.

New North American distributor:

SMC (formerly Samick Music Corp.)
18521 Railroad Street
City of Industry, California 91748

626-964-4700
800-592-9393
www.bechstein.de

Korean piano maker Samick has purchased a majority interest in C. Bechstein by acquiring the shares held by Karl Schulze, Bechstein's largest shareholder. Schulze also purchased a fifteen percent interest in Samick. Samick will help Bechstein increase production, diversify its product line, and sell in North America, and Bechstein will help Samick improve technically and market its pianos in Europe. Bechstein will remain as a separately managed German corporation.

Bechstein has introduced a new series of very beautiful designer verticals called "ProBechstein" in 45½", 46½", and 49" sizes. In the Pricing Guide section, they are the models called "Balance," "Avance," and "Ars Nova."

The 9' 2" model D-280 concert grand has been redesigned, with a capo bar and duplex scale in the treble for better tonal projection and tonal color. Also, unlike most other Bechsteins, which utilize an open pinblock design, this concert grand plate covers the pinblock area. These features have also been added to the new 6' 4" model M/P-192 grand and the 6' 11" B-210. The 7' 7" C-232 remains unchanged for the time being.

SMC, Samick's North American distribution arm, will market and distribute Bechstein pianos in the U.S. and Canada. The verticals and grands mentioned above, plus the 51½" Concert 8 vertical, will be called the "Concert Series" and will say "C. Bechstein" on the fallboard. This line will use the best quality materials and receive the best voicing. The regular verticals and the older, unenhanced versions of the above grands, namely models A-160 (5' 3"), A-190 (6' 3"), and A-208 (6' 9"), will be known as the "Academy Series" and will say only "Bechstein" on the fallboard. The company says that materials for this lower-priced line will be "sourced worldwide for value." Manufacturing will be done at Bechstein plants in Germany and the Czech Republic. (The company says that contrary to rumor, none of the parts for these pianos will be sourced in Asia.)

The W. Hoffmann line of pianos has been discontinued in the U.S. and Canada.

BECKER, J.

Distribution of these pianos in the U.S. has been discontinued.

BEHNING

Distribution discontinued. See "Weber"

BEIJING XINGHAI (new listing)

Beijing Piano Factory, part of the Beijing Xinghai Musical Instruments Co., has been producing pianos since 1949 and manufactures more than fifty thousand vertical and grand pianos annually. They are available throughout the world under the Otto Meister and Xinghai labels, as well as under various other labels as joint ventures with other manufacturers and distributors, including Heintzmann (in Canada), Ellington (Baldwin), Story & Clark, and Wyman. Kawai also has a joint venture with Beijing, though the pianos are distributed only in Canada and Europe, not the U.S. (at one time they bore the name "Linden").

The assets of Canadian piano manufacturer Heintzman were purchased by a Chinese company and moved from Canada to Beijing, where pianos are now produced under the Heintzman name in joint venture with the Beijing Piano Factory by a firm known as Beijing Heintzman. Prices were not available at press time.

BERGMANN

See "Young Chang"

BLONDEL, G.

Distribution of Blondel pianos in the U.S. has been discontinued.

BLÜTHNER

In honor of the company's 150th anniversary, Blüthner has introduced a Jubilee model with a commemorative cast-iron plate in the style of the special-edition pianos of a century ago. Available only in model 6 (6' 3"), it can be ordered in any style and finish.

In what is perhaps a world's "first," Blüthner has designed and built a piano for left-handed pianists. This is a completely "backwards" piano, with the treble keys, hammers, and strings on the left and the bass on the right. When it was introduced, a pianist gave a concert on it after only a couple of hours of practice! It is currently available in the 6' 10" and 9' 2" sizes by special order (price not available).

BOHEMIA (new listing)

German American Trading, Inc.
P.O. Box 17789
Tampa, Florida 33682

813-961-8405
germanamer@aol.com

Pianos made by: Bohemia Piano Co., Hradec Kralove, Czech Republic

The factory that makes Bohemia pianos began production in 1871, after World War II becoming part of the Czech state-owned enterprise that included the better-known Petrof. Privatized in 1993, Bohemia now makes 2,000 verticals and 300 grands per year. Originally it exported to the U.S. under the name Rieger-Kloss (now discontinued). The name Bohemia is derived from the original term used by the ancient Romans for the part of Europe that is now the Czech Republic.

Specifications for the instruments include Czech solid spruce soundboards, Czech-made sand-cast plates, either Czech Detoa actions on Bohemia action frames or Renner parts on Bohemia action frames (the latter denoted by

"BR" in model numbers), and either Renner or Abel hammers. All pianos come with a leather upholstered adjustable artist bench, and the grands all have slow-close fallboards.

The Bohemia grands I played at a trade show sounded and felt very good, with a nice, bright, singing treble tone.

Warranty: Ten years, parts and labor.

BÖSENDORFER

New U.S. distributor address, phone, and e-mail:

Bösendorfer USA
P.O. Box 1130
Richland, Washington 99354

888-936-2516
info@bosendorferamerica.com

In January 2002, Bösendorfer was purchased from Kimball International by the BAWAG - P.S.K. Group, Austria's third largest banking group. Bösendorfer has a special place in Austrian history and culture, and although the company has thrived under Kimball's ownership, for some time there has been a desire on all sides to return Bösendorfer to Austrian hands. The new owner says it intends to maintain the same high standards of material and workmanship for which the company is renowned. It will also continue the new marketing course of the last few years, including the redesign of existing models, a new "Artisan" series of art case pianos, and the Conservatory series of cosmetically reduced, less expensive versions of its models.

In 2001, Bösendorfer introduced a new 9' 2" model 280 concert grand, and in 2002, a 6' 1" model 185 grand. These and other new and redesigned models share a new design philosophy in which the treble soundboard area is increased for better tonal projection by reducing excess cabinet distance between player and strings, and the bass soundboard area is increased for better bass response by joining the wide tail to the spine at a sharper corner. Action geometry has been improved, the company says, on all models. In 2005, a maple cap was added to the inside top edge of the bent side and tail of the model 280 rim. The company says the added rigidity and mass should increase the concert grand's tonal projection and sustain.

The new concert grand is in addition to the two other concert grands (9' and 9' 6") the company already produces. Unlike the others, however, which have 92 and 97 keys, respectively, this new model has only 88 keys. Its scale design also features a front duplex. The company says the new model is intended for concert pianists who would otherwise be distracted or intimidated by the presence of additional keys in the bass. To my ears, the new piano has better sustain in the treble than I usually find in Bösendorfer pianos, but otherwise has a characteristic Bösendorfer sound and feel. The 9' model 275 is now available only by special order.

Bösendorfer showed several new models in 2003: a Porsche-designed modern piano suggestive of an automobile, a Victorian-styled piano called "Vienna," and two 175th anniversary models limited to a production run of 175 instruments each. The anniversary models, 52" model 130 and 5' 8" model 175, have such cosmetic enhancements as a burl walnut fallboard, gold trim, and a numbered medallion. Aside from the cosmetic enhancements, model 175 is the equivalent of a model 170 in the Conservatory series (not normally offered in this size), except with a high polish finish instead of satin. In 2004, the Anniversary models were retired, but are still available by special order. The Conservatory series models described in *The Piano Book* are now limited to models 200 and 214.

The SE Reproducer system, out of production for a number of years, is being brought back in 2005 under the name "Zeus" with updated electronics and solenoids. Bösendorfer says that the library for it will have top performers and that the system will play other disc formats as well.

BOSTON

The 49" vertical model UP-125 has been replaced with a completely redesigned 50" model UP-126. In the redesign, the wooden back has been made much heftier and the plate much more rigid to better resist torsional and bending stresses. Similar changes have also been made to the 52" model UP-132E, and the 46" model UP-118E. In the two larger models, the bass scale has been reworked with reduced string tension for smoother bass tone, and the soundboard taper and rib placement have been refined for better treble tone. Lastly, the music desk for the European-style case design has been improved so that it holds music more securely. Boston says it has plans to redesign the grands over time using the same structural analysis software employed in the design of its Essex line of pianos.

In 2005, Boston replaced its 7' 2" model GP-218 with a newly redesigned 7' 1" model GP-215 grand. The company says that a modified rim shape and bracing, increased string length in the mid-treble, overall increased string tension, and other technical changes have resulted in a piano with better mid-range and treble sustain and more "bite" to the bass.

BREITMANN (new listing)

German Piano Imports LLC
5660 W. Grand River Ave.
Lansing, Michigan 48906

517-886-6000
800-954-3200
info@bluthnerpiano.com
www.bluthnerpiano.com

Pianos made by: Artfield Piano Ltd., Qing Pu, China

Breitmann is a brand associated with Blüthner and made in China. Features include Delignit pinblocks, laminated spruce soundboards, German strings, Abel hammers, and Renner parts in the grands.

THE BRITISH PIANO MANUFACTURING COMPANY LTD. (new listing)

This was, for a time, the new name for the company formerly known as Whelpdale, Maxwell & Codd. This company produced Welmar, Knight, Broadwood, Bentley, and Woodchester pianos. It purchased Woodchester in 2001 and moved the manufacturing facilities for all its brands to the Woodchester factory, formerly the Bentley factory (see *The Piano Book* for history).

In April, 2003, this company ceased operations. Its assets were purchased by a piano distributor in the United Kingdom, who said he has no immediate plans to reissue the brand names.

Clarification: In *The Piano Book* entry for Whelpdale Maxwell & Codd, I wrote that John Broadwood & Sons was established in 1728. It has been brought to my attention that this is not possible because Broadwood was not born until 1732. The 1728 (or 1729) date is widely used, however, and it probably represents the date of establishment of the shop of Burkat Shudi, with whom Broadwood apprenticed (1761), and of whose business Broadwood later became partner (1770) and, eventually, sole proprietor (1782).

CABLE, HOBART M.

See "Sejung"

CHASE, A. B. (new listing)

Musical Properties, Inc.
949 French Drive
Mundelein, Illinois 60060

773-342-4212

Pianos made by: Dongbei Piano Co., Dongbei, China

A. B. Chase is an old American piano name, formerly owned by Aeolian Pianos but to the best of my knowledge not used since that company's bankruptcy in 1985. Since 2001, the brand has been used by Musical Properties, Inc. on pianos from the Dongbei piano factory in China.

CHICKERING

See "Baldwin" and "Samick"

CONN

See "Krakauer"

DISKLAVIER

See "Yamaha"

EBEL, CARL

See "Perzina, Gebr."

ELLINGTON

See "Baldwin"

ESSEX

Steinway, through its Boston Piano Co. subsidiary, introduced several "Essex" models in early 2001 and 2002. These are manufactured in Korea by Young Chang. They include 5' 3" and 6' grands and 42" and 44" verticals. The vertical models are of identical scale design, but the smaller one is in a continental-style cabinet. Some of the vertical cabinets look backward to styles of past decades of the twentieth century. The grands are available in both traditional and Art Deco styles, the difference being in the styling of the music desk, and in a Chippendale style. Like Boston pianos, the Essex line was designed with a lower tension duplex scale and a larger, tapered solid spruce soundboard, for potentially better sustain. The grands utilize rosette-shaped flanges for better action stability. Steinway says it designed these pianos using state-of-the-art structural analysis software.

At press time, Steinway announced the beginning of a collaboration with Guangzhou Pearl River Piano Group. Steinway says that in early 2006 it will release several new Essex models made in China by Pearl River.

ESTONIA

In 2001, having purchased the remaining shares in the company from the company employees, the former majority owner became the sole owner of the company. The name of the company has been changed to reflect his ownership.

New U.S. distributor contact information:

Laul Estonia Piano Factory
7 Fillmore Drive
Stony Point, New York 10980

845-947-7763
laulestoniapiano@aol.com
www.laulestoniapiano.com

The company reports that it has made a large number of changes and improvements during the past three years, among which are: rescaling the bass and upgrading bass string making machinery; improving the method of drilling pinblocks; stronger plates and improved plate finishes; thicker inner rims on the 5' 6" grands; improved fitting of soundboard to rim; concert-grand-quality soundboard spruce on all models; quarter-sawn maple bridge caps; an adjustable duplex scale; wood for legs and keyslips treated to better resist moisture; Renner Blue hammers on all models; better quality metal hardware that resists oxidation; suede-covered music desk tray; improved satin finishes; establishing a quality control department headed by the elder Mr. Laul (both he and his wife are professional musicians); higher-grade and better-prepared veneers; and establishing a U.S. service center for warranty repairs. All pianos are now accompanied by a quality control certificate signed by a member of the Laul family.

Concerning the criticisms in *The Piano Book*, technicians report that Estonia pianos are now arriving at the dealer well-prepared, and seem not to have problems anymore with uneven tuning pin tightness. Based on technical improvements the company has made and new information from technicians,

I would raise both the "Confidence" and "Quality Control" ratings of Estonia pianos to four and a half stars (see *The Piano Book* for details about the rating system).

ETERNA

Distribution discontinued.

EVERETT

New distributor phone number: 800-445-0695

Most Everett models are made by the Dongbei Piano Co. in Dongbei, China. However, a few models are made by a different Chinese company, one that calls itself "Everett" and manufactures pianos under the Everett name for the domestic Chinese market.

FALCONE

See "Sejung"

FAZIOLI

Corrections to review: Three lids are optional on the 10' 2" grand. The 5' 2", 6', and 6' 11" models utilize a Delignit pinblock as mentioned, but the larger models have Bolduc (Canadian) pinblocks. The Fazioli warranty has been increased to ten years.

Additional web site address: www.fazioli.com

FEURICH

New U.S. representative:

Unique Pianos, Inc.
159 Parkhill Blvd.
Melbourne, Florida 32904

888-725-6633
321-725-5690
www.feurich.com

Pianos made by: Feurich Klavier-u.Flügelfabrikation GmbH, Gunzenhausen, Germany

This venerable German manufacturer is once again making pianos in its own factory. The models being offered at this time are 5' 8" (F172) and 7' 5" (F227) grands and a 49" (F123) vertical.

FÖRSTER, AUGUST

New web site address: www.august-foerster.de

GROTRIAN

Grotrian now distributes directly from the factory:

Grotrian Piano Company
P.O. Box 5833
D-38049 Braunschweig, Germany

49-531-210100
49-531-2101040 (fax)
contact@grotrian.de
www.grotrian.de

The "Friedrich Grotrian" is a new 43-1/2" vertical with a beech back frame but no back posts, and a simpler cabinet, at a lower price than regular Grotrian pianos.

Grotrian has introduced the Duo Grand Piano, two grand pianos placed side by side with keyboards at opposite ends, as in a duo piano concert, with removable rim parts, connected soundboards, and a common lid (price not available).

GULBRANSEN (new listing)

QRS Music Technologies, Inc.
2011 Seward Avenue
Naples, Florida 34109

800-247-6557
www.gulbransen.com

Pianos made by: Sejung Corp., Qingdao, China

Founded in 1904, Gulbransen was a well-regarded piano and organ manufacturer of the early twentieth century, and at one time was the world's largest maker of player pianos. In more modern times, the company was known for its electronic organs and MIDI products. In 2004, QRS Music

Technologies, maker of the Pianomation player piano systems and distributor of Story & Clark pianos, purchased Gulbransen's MIDI products and company name.

QRS is using an innovative distribution strategy to market Gulbransen pianos. In addition to selling through regular piano dealers, QRS is also selling the pianos online through its own web site (see above) and through Amazon.com at a fixed, non-negotiable price. Piano teachers and technicians may also take orders. Regardless of who sells the piano, if there is a participating QRS dealer in the customer's area, that dealer will provide delivery and after-sale support and will earn the profit from the sale, less a commission to the seller. If there is no participating dealer in the area, QRS will provide delivery and support directly from its national headquarters.

Currently the Gulbransen line consists of two sizes of grand, both with and without player systems, and two sizes of vertical, made by Sejung. The pianos are tuned, inspected, and adjusted at the Story & Clark facility in Pennsylvania prior to being shipped to the dealer or customer.

HALLET, DAVIS & CO.

The Dongbei Piano Co. is now making many of the Hallet & Davis pianos from China.

HAZELTON BROS.

See "Samick"

HEINTZMAN

See "Beijing Xinghai"

HOFFMANN, W.

See "Bechstein, C."

IBACH

New U.S. distributor information:

Resource West, Inc.
2295 E. Sahara Avenue
Las Vegas, Nevada 89104

702-457-7919
800-777-6874
info@ibachpiano.com
www.ibachpiano.com

The real German Ibach pianos are once again being distributed in the United States. Resource West says it will be distributing these fine pianos through interior design professionals and some smaller piano dealers. No investment is needed by the dealer. In lieu of stocking the pianos and receiving a regular retail markup, the dealer instead refers interested customers to the Resource West/Ibach showroom in Las Vegas and receives a substantial commission when a sale is made. Resource West prepares the pianos and delivers them to the customers. The price list in this *Supplement* is the suggested retail price at the Las Vegas showroom.

The Ibach-Daewoo joint venture mentioned in *The Piano Book* was discontinued and the Korean manufacturing operation was sold by Daewoo to an investment group that continued to manufacture pianos in Korea on a limited basis. These pianos were distributed for a time in the U.S. under the name Bachendorff (an arrangement now discontinued) and in Canada under the name Royale. A distributor operating under the name Persis International, Inc. says it will be having this Korean company make pianos under the Sohmer name (see "Sohmer").

IRMLER

The Chinese-made Irmlers have been discontinued. The European Irmlers are made in Poland with the technological assistance of Blüthner. Final action assembly and regulation is performed in the Blüthner factory in Germany.

KAWAI
including Shigeru Kawai

Additional web site address: www.shigerukawai.com

Kawai has opened a factory in Indonesia, where it is making many of the piano models sold in the U.S. The company is in the process of closing its North Carolina plant and moving all its U.S. manufacturing to Indonesia. Kawai also produces several vertical models in joint venture with the Beijing Xinghai Piano Co. in China. These pianos are known as the KX models, and are sold in Canada and Europe, but not in the U.S. At one time these pianos bore the name "Linden," but use of that name has been discontinued.

True to its reputation, Kawai has made even more changes to its product line. The model 505 and 605 furniture-style consoles have been discontinued and replaced with several 44½" and 45" models utilizing the same scale design as the 605. Model 506 is this piano in a simple, studio-style cabinet, made in Indonesia. Although called a "studio" because of the cabinet style, it has a compressed action characteristic of a console. Model 508 is the same as the 506, except with a slightly fancier cabinet. Model 606, recently discontinued, is the same design in a U.S.-made furniture-style console; model 608 is also the same design internally with a fancier Indonesian-made cabinet. These models now are all made in Kawai's own factory in Indonesia.

Popular studio models UST-7 and UST-8 are also now being made in Indonesia, although U.S.-made versions will remain in stock for some time. The 46½" furniture-style studio model 902 has been changed to model 906, with a stiffer back structure, all ABS action parts, and new cabinetry. UST-10 and UST-12 are, respectively, 48" and 52" American-style institutional (school) uprights, similar internally to the K-25 and K-60 uprights. Models 906, UST-10, and UST-12, formerly made in North Carolina, will continue to be sold while supplies last.

Among the Japanese-made models, model K-18 is the 506 in a Japanese-style, polyester-finished cabinet. It replaces the recent CX-10 and its predecessor, the popular model CX-5H, as Kawai's low-priced "studio." Model K-25 is like the 48" model K-30 (discontinued), except in a simpler cabinet.

Kawai has invented a variable-touch action for vertical pianos in which the player can vary the touchweight by sliding a lever. The lever operates a set of sliding weights behind the fallboard. The touchweight varies depending on the point at which the keys contact the sliding weights. The touchweight can be adjusted from 48 to 70 grams (normal for Kawai is 56 grams). The "Vari-Touch" feature is currently available only on the 52" K-60 upright (model VT-132).

In the grands, the 5' model GM-2A has become model GM-10, which is further divided into two levels of cabinetry. The GM-10C is the original GM-10, with a non-movable music desk (a nuisance) and a plain cabinet. This model has recently been discontinued. The GM-10LE is an upgraded version, with a movable music desk and a nicer cabinet. The 5' 1" model GE-1A has been replaced by the GE-20, which has the features of the former

GE-1AS model. A new 5' 5" model GE-30 has been introduced. It has the same scale as the model RX-1, but is like the other GE models structurally and in terms of its features (see *The Piano Book* for details on the differences between the RX, GE, and GM models).

As explained in *The Piano Book*, Kawai uses ABS Styran plastic as the material for many of its action parts. In 2004, the company introduced a new generation of these parts, which it calls the "Millennium III" action, made of ABS Styran mixed with carbon fibers. The carbon fibers allow the parts to be more rigid with less weight and to be more finely engineered for shape and texture, resulting in a faster, lighter action and more consistent touch. I played two pianos of identical model, one with the older parts and one with the new, and could sense a substantial difference. At present, the new parts are found in the RX and Shigeru Kawai grands.

From time to time, Kawai makes available several of their grand and upright models in limited quantity as "Conservatory" and "Promotional" versions. The Conservatory model uprights have a wider music rack than the regular models, usually larger or double casters and a lock, and sometimes cabinetry or aesthetics that are slightly simplified. Promotional models have a regular (not soft-fall) fallboard and some other simplified features. Prices were not available at press time, but are expected to be about the same or slightly less than regular models.

Kawai's high-end Shigeru Kawai line of pianos is now available in six different models from 5' 10" to 9' 1". New for 2005 are two special finishes in the Shigeru VII (7' 6") – Pyramid Mahogany and Classic Noblesse (with inlaid walnut burl).

KEMBLE

Kemble is now acting as its own distributor for the U.S. The factory contact information is:

Kemble & Company Ltd.
Mount Avenue
Bletchley, Milton Keynes MK1 1JE
United Kingdom

44-1908-371771
44-1908-270448 (fax)
brian_kemble@gmx.yamaha.com
www.kemble-pianos.co.uk

The 43" "Oxford" is now available with a beautiful marquetry inlay. A new 46½" "Windsor" model has been added to the Kemble line, and the "Traditional" model has been discontinued. The 52" model K131 vertical, formerly available only as a limited-edition designer model, is now available as a regular model. There is also a new 48" Shaker-styled designer upright called "Vermont" designed by the famous British designers Conran and Partners, a 45" black polyester and chrome model called "Classic-T," and a 49" model called "Quantum II" with a sound-escape mechanism.

Kemble has introduced its first grand piano, a 5' 8" "Conservatoire" model, in cooperation with Yamaha, which owns a majority interest in Kemble. The grand is like the Yamaha model C2, with design differences such as plate color and music desk shape. It is also voiced to Kemble's specs, sounding to me more "European," i.e. a mellower bass.

KIMBALL

Brighton Music, Inc.
1155 W. 4ᵗʰ Street, Suite 214
Reno, Nevada 89503

773-342-4212

As described in *The Piano Book*, Kimball International ceased making pianos in 1996 and has stated that it has no plans to reintroduce Kimball brand pianos. The trademarked name has been registered by a different distributor and is being used once again. A prototype piano was seen at a recent trade show, but few details were available as to country of origin or specifications. The distributor said that a full line of pianos and complete details would be available in Fall 2005.

KINGSBURG

This brand is no longer being distributed in the U.S.

KLIMA (new listing)

Klima was a small Czech piano manufacturer established in 1991 when the state-run piano manufacturing apparatus was sold off to several private firms, including Petrof. Several generations of the Klima family had been Petrof employees. Klima pianos were distributed in the United States for a brief period of time before the company discontinued production in 2004.

Klima vertical pianos are also available under the Fandrich & Sons label with a Fandrich vertical action installed. See *The Piano Book* for details and contact information.

KNABE, WM.

The Wm. Knabe piano line made by Young Chang for PianoDisc has been discontinued, and PianoDisc has licensed the name to Samick. Samick is now using this name on the pianos formerly sold as the "World Piano" premium line of Samick pianos (see *The Piano Book* for details). Gradually the grands are being redesigned, the new models based on the original nineteenth and early twentieth century Knabe scale designs and cabinet styles in use when the company was based in Baltimore, with sand-cast plates, lacquer finishes, Renner actions and hammers, maple and oak rim, and other high quality features. At present, this redesign has resulted in the 5' 8" (WKG-58) and 6' 4" (WKG-64) models, with the other grand models still based on the World Piano series. The pianos are serviced in Samick's Los Angeles facility before being shipped to dealers.

I have watched the Knabe line develop over the last couple of years and have noted many improvements. Some of these improvements are the result of collaboration with Bechstein engineers in the Samick factory. The instruments I have played have been impressive, especially for a Korean-made piano. I also made inquiry among my sources around the country. The pianos arrive in very good condition cosmetically. Most are also well-prepared technically, though not always. In a few cases, technicians found it necessary to completely re-weight the keyboard after correctly regulating the action. A few pianos in bone-dry regions have experienced structural and mechanical problems in the winter, including cracked soundboards. The dealers diligently repaired or replaced the affected pianos, and Samick responded by switching soundboard suppliers to avoid further problems. Other parts of the country did not report problems. When well prepared, most observers thought the pianos to be very musical, well designed, and a good value. For the time being, I would recommend paying special attention to humidity control in dry climates.

KRAKAUER

U.S. distribution of Krakauer and Conn pianos is temporarily being handled by the manufacturer's Hong Kong office while the company is seeking a new distributor. Prices are not available at this time.

MASON & HAMLIN

In 2004, Mason & Hamlin reintroduced its 6' 4" model AA grand piano, a model the company manufactured during the first half of the twentieth century. The current version is modified somewhat from the old, but does have features typical of the company's other models, such as a wide tail, a full-perimeter plate, and the patented "tension resonator" crown retention system. In the process of developing the model, the company says, it standardized certain features, refined manufacturing processes, and modernized jigs and machinery, improvements that will now be applied to the other models the company makes. Other technical refinements to the grands include reducing mass in the action and tapering the soundboard. I played a prototype of the AA at a trade show and think it has the potential for becoming the company's most popular model.

In January 2005, the company reintroduced the 9' 4" model CC Concert Grand, not produced since 1984. It has the same features typical of the company's other models. However, its length requires the use of a double tension resonator.

The model 50 vertical piano has been redesigned, with longer keys for a more grand-like touch and improved pedal leverage. A satin ebony cabinet will be available in 2005.

McPHAIL (new listing)

McPhail Piano Ltd.
796 Boston Post Road
Marlboro, Massachusetts 01752

866-MCPHAIL (627-4245)
www.auditionapiano.com

Pianos made by: Sejung Corp., Qingdao, China

McPhail is the name of an old Boston-based piano manufacturer from the late eighteenth and early nineteenth centuries. The current McPhail Piano Ltd. was founded in the Boston area in 2003. Pianos are available on a rent to own basis and are marketed through "partners" — music stores, piano teachers, and schools — but not through regular piano dealerships. The "Audition Program" was developed to offer beginners a new instrument with proper touch and tone, but with low investment risk, as an alternative to a used piano or electric keyboard.

Customers "audition" (rent) a McPhail piano for six months, after which they may return the instrument or purchase it with all rent payments credited toward the purchase price. The company arranges all preparation, delivery, and contractual matters.

Presently, McPhail offers 44" consoles and 47" studios in various cabinet designs and 5' and 5' 4" grands. Monthly rental charges range from $75 to $95 for verticals and $175 to $225 for grands. All McPhail pianos feature solid spruce soundboards, sand-cast plates, and maple action parts and come with a twelve-year parts/ten-year labor warranty. The pianos are currently manufactured by Sejung in China.

MEISTER, OTTO

See "Beijing Xinghai"

MILLER, HENRY F. (new listing)

Henry F. Miller
236 West Portal Ave. #568
San Francisco, California 94127

info@henryfmiller.com

This is the name of an old American piano maker dating back to 1863, no longer in business. The name is now owned by the Sherman Clay chain of piano stores. Current Henry F. Miller pianos are made by Pearl River in China and are similar to pianos sold under the Pearl River name. However, the company says in the future it may source these pianos from a variety of Asian manufacturers. The pianos are sold in Sherman Clay, Jordan Kitt's, and other major piano retailers throughout the country.

NIENDORF

No longer in production

NORDISKA

Nordiska has introduced several new grand and vertical models. All models have Abel hammers except the 43" model 109 console.

A new Master Series of redesigned grands utilizes a focused beam structure that concentrates the piano's structural support toward the nose flange of the plate, a design used by Steinway and others that is thought to increase the tonal projection of the instrument by making the frame more rigid; and a maple rim, heavier plate, and better plate cosmetics. This series includes the 6' 1" model 185 M, 7' model 215, and 9' model 275. The 7' and 9' grands also feature a Bolduc (Canadian) white spruce soundboard, full Renner action, and Kluge keys. Model 185 is available in both Master Series and regular versions. The 7' grand has an especially good sound and touch, the best yet on a Chinese-made piano. The company says that imported American veneers are being used on all grands.

PALATINO (new listing)

The Music Link
P.O. Box 162
Brisbane, California 94005

888-552-5465
piano@palatinousa.com
www.palatinousa.com

Pianos made by: AXL Musical Instruments Co., Ltd. Corp., Shanghai, China

Although this company is new to the piano world, it is not new to music. For some time, AXL has been manufacturing a full range of musical instruments under its own name and under OEM agreements with other companies. The company says that its factory is very automated, employing CNC routers from Japan and Germany, and that it sources materials for the pianos from around the world.

At present the company makes three sizes of vertical piano and three sizes of grand. Specifications include solid spruce soundboard on verticals, laminated spruce soundboard on grands, hard rock maple pinblock and bridges, adjustable artist bench with all models, and a ten-year transferable warranty. A slow-close fallboard is standard on grands, but by special order only on verticals.

Several verticals I inspected at a trade show were definitely better than the average piano from China and had apparently arrived in excellent condition, needing hardly any preparation. It seems this was not an isolated case, as other people are starting to report similar observations. This is a brand to watch.

PEARL RIVER
including Ritmüller

New contact information for U.S. distributor:

Pearl River Piano Group America, Ltd.
2260 S. Haven Avenue, Suite F
Ontario, California 91761

909-673-9155
800-435-5086
sales@pearlriverusa.com
www.pearlriverpiano.com

Pearl River has added 5' 7" and 6' 4" grands to its line. The company says these models are scaled to sound like Japanese or American pianos, whereas the other models are more European sounding. The 7' and 9' Pearl River grands now come with Renner actions. The company is in the process of changing the specifications of the 7' and 9' Pearl River and Ritmüller grands to include solid spruce soundboards; all other Ritmüller grands will follow in 2006.

A 49" vertical model 126R has been added to the Ritmüller line. The vertical is based on the model 125M1 joint venture piano (with Yamaha), but with agraffes throughout the scale. Renner action is standard on the 7' Ritmüller grand, and available at additional cost on the smaller models.

PERZINA, GEBR. (new listing)

Piano Empire, Inc.
13370 E. Firestone Blvd., Ste. A
Santa Fe Springs, California 90670

800-576-3463
562-926-1906
info@perzinapianos.com
www.perzinapianos.com

Pianos made by: Yantai-Perzina Piano Manufacturing Co., Ltd., Yantai, China. Some names formerly made by Yantai Longfeng Piano Co.

Names used: Gebr. Perzina, Carl Ebel, Gerh. Steinberg.

The Gebr. Perzina (Brothers Perzina) piano company was established in the German town of Schwerin in 1871, and was a prominent piano maker until World War I, after which its fortunes declined. In more recent times, the factory was moved to the nearby city of Lenzen and the company is now known as Pianofabrik Lenzen GmbH. In the early 1990s, the company was purchased by Music Brokers International B.V. in The Netherlands. Eventually it was decided that making pianos in Germany was not economically viable, so manufacturing was moved to Yantai, China, where a range of verticals and grands were made for a number of years by the Yantai Longfeng Piano Co. under the Perzina name. In 2003, Music Brokers International established its own factory in Yantai, called Yantai-Perzina Piano Manufacturing Co. Ltd., where it now builds the Perzina, Carl Ebel, and Gerh. Steinberg pianos. (Note: Do not confuse Gerh. Steinberg with Wilh. Steinberg, a German piano brand.)

The Carl Ebel and Gerh. Steinberg pianos are based on the same scale design, but the Perzina scale design is different. Further technical differences revolve primarily around the choice of action, hammers, and soundboard design, among other things. In particular, the Perzina brand is distinguished by use of a solid, tapered, Austrian white spruce soundboard in both verticals and grands, whereas the Carl Ebel and Gerh. Steinberg soundboards are of Sitka spruce in the grands and veneered laminated spruce in the verticals. In addition, the Perzina verticals have several interesting features rarely found in other pianos, including a "floating" soundboard that is unattached to the back at certain points for freer vibration, and a reverse, or concave, soundboard crown. (There may be something to this, as the Perzina verticals are the best sounding verticals from China, the bass being particularly notable.) The Perzina grands are available with either Detoa ("G" models) or Renner ("E" models) action. The company says that the Perzina pianos also receive a higher level of attention to detail at the end of the manufacturing process than do the other two brands.

The company's European headquarters says it ships many European materials to Yantai, including Roslau strings, Delignit pinblocks, Abel hammers, English felts, European veneers, and Austrian white spruce soundboards. New machinery is from Germany, Japan and Italy. According to the company, all the piano designs are the original German scales. The Renner actions used in some of the Perzina grands are ordered complete from Germany, not assembled from parts.

PETROF
including Weinbach

Web site address: www.petrof.com

Petrof has introduced a new concert grand called the "P1 Mistral." The company says the instrument utilizes a more rigid brace and frame, front and rear duplex scales, and a Renner action, among other features. Also new is a 53" vertical model P135. It has a Renner action, full sostenuto, a soft-close fallboard, and a newly-designed adjustable music desk, among other features. Several of the vertical models are now available with designer panels with inlays.

All Petrof grands are now being shipped with Abel hammers. They should be easier to voice than the harder hammers previously used. Consequently, piano shoppers are now more likely to find individual Petrof grands with a mellower tone.

Petrof has designed new grand and vertical actions. Called "Petrof Original," the vertical action is currently being installed into new pianos, with the grand action coming soon. The geometry in the action for the model 115 vertical has been re-designed to function more like the larger verticals, i.e. a full-sized jack and longer hammer shank. Several of the parts, both grand and vertical, have been re-designed to achieve greater rigidity and less weight. The actions are being manufactured in a separate section of the Detoa factory under supervision by Petrof engineers. They can be identified by a "Petrof Original" label on the action.

Petrof has also invented a version of its new grand action, the "Magnetic Accelerated Action," that uses tiny opposing magnets on the wippens and wippen rail. These magnets allow for the removal of the usual lead counterweights in the keys and, according to the company, significantly alters the dynamic properties of the action. "The hammer receives an inertial boost from the magnets as the key begins to move from the rest position. When the key is fully depressed, the effect of the magnets is minimal, allowing gravity to work in giving the hammer another inertial boost on the way down. The effect is faster repetition, less fatigue, and less physical work needed to reach higher dynamic levels." The new action also furthers the European Union's stated environmental goal of phasing out the use of lead in pianos. The action is adjusted in the factory for a standard touchweight. If necessary, it can be adjusted up or down 5 grams by a technician (not the customer) in an hour or so. Otherwise, the action can (and should) be serviced in exactly the same way as a standard action. The Magnetic Accelerated Action is an option on all Petrof (but not Weinbach) grands.

PIANODISC

PianoDisc has replaced the PDS 128 Plus system with the 228 CFX. The main difference is that the 228 CFX has both a floppy drive and a CD drive as standard equipment, so it is unnecessary to plug in your own CD player (although you can do so if you have a multi-disc CD changer you want to use). The company says that the control box is the smallest such box with both floppy and CD drives on the market. It can be mounted on the piano or can be located up to 100 feet away and operated with the included infrared wireless remote control.

PianoDisc has introduced an MX Platinum option that utilizes 64 MB of flash memory to store hours of music and play it back without ever having to change a disk. MX Platinum comes with 35 hours of pre-selected music (589 songs), to which one can add music from floppy disks, TFT MIDI Record, and standard MIDI files (but not PianoDisc CDs). PianoDisc's regular MX feature with 32 MB of flash memory still remains available as an option.

The GT360 and GT90 QuietTime systems have been discontinued and replaced with a QuietTime system that includes most of the same components, but without the sound card and control box. The new system comes with a power supply, MIDI cable, a MIDI strip for installing under the keys, three pedal switches, a MIDI board with cover, headphones, and a mute rail that, when activated, prevents the hammers from hitting the strings. Customers can buy and use any off-the-shelf sound module with the system.

A question often arises concerning the relationship of the PianoDisc system components to the QuietTime system. The answer is that if you purchase the PianoDisc playback system with the SymphonyPro Sound Module, the TFT MIDI Record system, and the PianoMute Rail, you have purchased virtually all the components of the QuietTime system and have therefore acquired the QuietTime system virtually "free." The separate listing for QuietTime in the price list is for those who wish to purchase it without the PianoDisc playback. Those people will need to purchase, in addition, a sound module from their music dealer.

PianoDisc has introduced a new remote control called the PianoDisc Home Theater Master. It features an LCD touch screen and eliminates the need to have multiple remote controls to operate other various electronic devices. This remote is specially programmed to operate the PianoDisc and can be programmed to control eleven other Audio and Video components including: Stereo, CD, Tape, CATV, Satellite, TV, DVD, VCR and Laser Disc.

Note Release Control (NRC) has been developed by PianoDisc to reduce noise made by the keys when they are released. This is achieved by pulsing the solenoid during key release to slow the key down. This new feature is compatible with all PDS 128+ and 228 CFX Silent Drive systems, and is added by using the Flash Memory feature that allows for convenient software upgrades. To add NRC at no charge, get the PianoDisc Update 4.2 and Silent Drive CPU Update F from the PianoDisc web site or from an authorized PianoDisc installer.

For a limited time, PianoDisc is offering five hundred dollars in free music software with each PianoDisc system purchased. See your dealer for details.

The next generation PianoDisc system, Opus7, has just been released in 2004. In addition to the PianoDisc playback system and SymphonyPro sound module, Opus7 features a wireless, internet-ready, Web Tablet with touchscreen and full color, high resolution graphics as the system's "Conductor." It has the ability to download music and system upgrades directly from PianoDisc's website, and surf the web and receive email (broadband users only), among other features. The Opus7 system is invisible — mounted completely out of sight under the piano — but with an access panel that allows the user to connect the included floppy and CD drives for copying music to the system's "MX3" music storage hard drive beginning at 20-gigabytes in size. The MX3 hard drive comes with forty hours of pre-loaded music. Its MX3 media format will accept Standard MIDI files type 0 and 1 available from a wide variety of Standard MIDI file publishers, PianoDisc CDs, and standard audio CDs. (The company says while playback of non-PianoDisc media is supported, it is not guaranteed.) Music saved to the MX3 hard drive from diverse sources can be organized into separate "libraries" and played back from a single source for convenience. The MX3 format provides many hours of true digital stereo sound with piano accompaniment without having to change CDs. Music can also be purchased online from PianoDisc's new "eMusic" store and downloaded directly to the Opus7 and permanently stored on the MX3 hard drive.

Several new features were introduced in 2005. "PianoSync" is a MIDI-controlled piano performance that synchronizes with a commercially-available audio CD of a major recording artist. When you purchase a PianoSync performance from PianoDisc's growing collection, PianoDisc will recognize the matching audio CD and accompany the original recording on your piano whenever the CD is played. Both can be copied to MX3 for more convenient playback.

Using "PianoCast" and broadband internet, Opus7 can now connect to PianoDisc's internet radio station. The station will feature special events, interviews, and performances, combining a traditional audio broadcast with a piano performance that will play the Opus7.

Opus7 comes in two versions, "Opulence" and "Luxury." Opulence is the full system. Luxury is designed to integrate with home automation systems, and so does not come with the web tablet, router, or floppy and CD drives, as it is assumed that the home automation system will already include these or similar interfaces. A "Performance Package" option includes the TFT MIDI record strip, mute rail, and headphones for recording one's own playing or for use as a QuietTime system or MIDI controller. Owners of 228 CFX or PDS 128 PianoDisc systems can upgrade to Opus7 at a modest discount to the full system price. Note, however, that PianoDisc will continue to produce and sell the (current) 228 CFX system. Opus7 is distributed through an exclusive network of authorized dealers.

PianoDisc has reintroduced the AudioForte system, originally developed by Schimmel and described in an earlier edition of *The Piano Book*. AudioForte is a system of specialized speaker drivers mounted under the piano that turn a piano soundboard into spectacular stereo speakers.

PLEYEL

New U.S. representative:

Vince Grantano
7 MacArthur Blvd.
Apt. N 1111
Westmont, New Jersey 08108

Vgrantano@aol.com
www.pleyel.fr

The Pleyel factory currently employs about 85 workers, who build about 1,300 vertical pianos and 50 grands a year using a blend of high-tech machinery and hand craftsmanship. The company says it is concentrating on increasing exports, particularly in the niche for artcase and custom-made instruments. The first of these was the 47" vertical model P118 in luxury leather. The latest is the 6' 3" model P190 grand in bird's-eye poplar. Other new models include a new line of contemporary verticals, a 5' 8" model P170 grand, and a 9' 2" model 280 concert grand. The concert grand has white keytops made of mammoth bones, comparable in feel to ivory.

PRAMBERGER

See "Young Chang" and "Samick"

QRS / PIANOMATION

New phone number (change of area code): 239-597-5888

QRS has made changes to its line of Pianomation player piano systems since publication of the Fourth Edition of *The Piano Book*. As mentioned in the book, Pianomation consists of a basic MIDI-compatible playback engine common to all its systems plus a choice of several different front-end controllers that determine the input to the system.

The simplest and least expensive controller is the model 2000C. The control box is hidden under the piano. It has no built-in disk drives, but instead uses your own off-the-shelf stereo components to play QRS CDs and DVDs. The background music comes from your own stereo system, while a wireless transmitter sends the piano data to the Pianomation system, even through walls.

The model 2000CD+ is like the 2000C, above, but has a visible profile of two inches and includes its own CD drive for playing audio CDs. It is most often installed with an optional speaker. Because of its "plug and play" simplicity, it is the easiest to use and most popular of the systems.

New to the line are two "Petine" controllers. The first, Petine CD, is just over one and a half inches tall, and includes both a DVD ROM drive and a compact flash reader. The drive will play both audio CDs and data CDs (CD ROMs), the latter potentially containing thousands of MIDI files on a single CD. Control is by means of a data wheel and a three-digit LED display. There is also an external infrared sensor port, making it possible to install this controller out of sight while retaining the remote control capability. Petine CD also has a microphone input for karaoke and a 1.44 megabyte internal memory storage capacity. On board but not yet implemented are dual USB ports and an S-video output, the latter in order to provide eventual DVD capability. The operating system is flash upgradeable.

The second Petine controller, called "Petine Lite," is only one inch high. It includes everything Petine CD has except the disc drive, making it a practical choice for integrating with your own off-the-shelf stereo components or computer.

Also new to the line is the "Ancho" controller, which replaces the top of the line Analog-to-MIDI controller known as "Chili." Ancho has a 20-character

37

alpha-numeric display, unique among Pianomation controllers. It comes with both a DVD ROM drive and compact flash reader. The drive will play both audio CDs and data CDs (CD ROMs). This controller will also play Standard MIDI files types 1 and 0. It also has a microphone input for karaoke, a 1.44 megabyte internal memory storage capacity, a sound card, dual headphone outputs, and is most often installed with an optional speaker.

Ancho has both mixed and unmixed audio outputs so that the background music track and the piano track can be mixed for piping around the house, but the piano track can be omitted from the speakers located in the room containing the piano. Individual sources of audio sound can be finely adjusted so they will sound properly balanced at any volume level. Like the Petine controllers, Ancho has two onboard features, dual USB ports and an S-video output, that will be implemented with future upgrades. The operating system is flash upgradeable.

The above systems can be ordered or installed through any dealer doing business with QRS, but the company also makes two "Serenade" systems that are available only through an exclusive dealer network. Serenade CD is less than an inch high (for those who prefer their Pianomation to be as unobtrusive as possible) and has a CD ROM drive. It comes with a remote control.

Serenade Pro is a fully-loaded system similar to Ancho, with a CD (audio and CD ROM) drive, a sound module, record strip, and speaker, but also contains a hard drive (instead of internal memory) and a 900 mhz two-way wireless remote, has space for an optional karaoke card, and will play MP3 (live music) files. It does not have Ancho's capability for both mixed and unmixed audio outputs and headphone jacks.

Sync-Along is a new feature that will play on Ancho, Petine, or Serenade Pro. QRS has prepared a piano track in MIDI format, stored in internal memory, to go along with each of a number of popular audio CDs and DVDs available on the general market. When the owner plays the CD or DVD, Sync-Along links it with the stored piano track, enabling Pianomation to accurately play along with the CD or DVD. A new Transcription series is similar to Sync-Along but without the background music or visual accompaniment. A solo performance audio CD is transcribed and offered as a Pianomation CD so the customer can hear the performance on his or her own piano.

The QRS record option used to be offered in both "LiteSwitch" and "OptiScan" versions. These have been discontinued. QRS is currently using the well-regarded Gulbransen record strip while it is developing a new generation of the OptiScan record system.

QRS has introduced its "NetPiano" service through which customers can download any of the thousands of songs from the QRS library to their Pianomation-equipped piano through their personal computer. A wireless transmitter plugged into the computer's audio jack transmits the music to the piano. The service is subscription based, and allows the customer to have access to songs anytime, day or night, without having to build their own CD library. Subscriptions are available only through QRS dealers or through the QRS web site.

QRS also has available an optional tablet remote control with a Media Player plug-in, with which the user can control Pianomation, access NetPiano, or surf the web, via the user's computer, from anywhere in the home.

Jukebox Kiosk is a product for commercial establishments. It contains the entire QRS library, updated continuously, from which customers can choose individual songs to play for a small fee.

Apart from its player piano systems, QRS is constantly inventing new gadgets and gizmos for pianos that can be installed independently of Pianomation. Recent inventions include a Grand Mute Rail for quieting the sound of a grand piano (these have existed for verticals before, but not for grands), and a Grand Fallboard Closer that allows a grand fallboard to close gently and avoid hurting the player's fingers (available on many new pianos for some time, but not previously as an add-on accessory).

QRS has acquired the exclusive rights to manufacture and sell a Self-Tuning Piano System (which does not yet have a trade name). The company says the system will be designed into the manufacture of a piano and will allow the piano to maintain itself in tune between major tunings by a piano tuner. The system works by heating each string slightly to change its pitch. Initially the piano is tuned slightly sharp. While the system senses the pitch of each string, a tiny heating element under each string will heat it very slightly until it is lowered to the correct pitch. When the piano can no longer be tuned in this manner, it will need a regular tuning. It is expected that the system will be of particular interest to institutions. It was invented by Don A. Gilmore of Kansas City, Missouri. [This interesting-sounding system is temporarily on hold while the bugs are being worked out.]

REMINGTON

See "Samick"

RIDGEWOOD

Weber Piano Co., distributor of Ridgewood pianos, has gone out of business, and with it has gone the Ridgewood name. See "Weber."

RIEGER-KLOSS

The Rieger-Kloss line of pianos has been discontinued. The Bohemia Piano Co. is now making and distributing pianos under its own name. See under "Bohemia" in this section for more information.

RITMÜLLER

See under "Pearl River"

SAGENHAFT

Weber Piano Co., distributor of Sagenhaft pianos, has gone out of business, and with it has gone the Sagenhaft name. See "Weber."

SAMICK
including Kohler & Campbell, Conover Cable, Hazelton Bros., Remington, Pramberger, and others

New web site address: www.smcmusic.com

Samick Music Corporation, the North American marketing arm of the Korean company, is now known as SMC, and distributes Samick, Kohler & Campbell, Conover Cable, Hazelton Bros., Pramberger, Remington, Wm. Knabe (see "Knabe, Wm."), and Sohmer & Co. (see "Sohmer") pianos in North America. Under an arrangement with Baldwin, SMC temporarily distributed Chickering pianos left over from a production run never claimed and paid for by Baldwin after its bankruptcy (see "Baldwin"). Samick has also recently acquired a majority interest in the C. Bechstein company, a major German manufacturer. See under "Bechstein, C." Samick is no longer making pianos under the Bernhard Steiner name.

In March 2004, Samick acquired a controlling interest in its competitor Young Chang, and SMC briefly took over distribution of Young Chang and Bergmann pianos in the United States. However, court rulings in Korea and the United States at least temporarily ended this arrangement in March 2005, pending further litigation. At press time, Young Chang and Bergmann pianos are once again being distributed by Young Chang's U.S. distributor, AND Music Corporation (see "Young Chang" for details).

Samick has acquired the rights to the Pramberger name. Pramberger was a name used by Young Chang under license from piano engineer Joseph Pramberger. When Mr. Pramberger died in 2003, his estate had the opportunity to terminate its relationship with Young Chang and did so. Samick quickly licensed the rights to the Pramberger name. However, Young Chang still holds the rights to the original designs, so Samick is designing new pianos to go with the name. A "J.P. Pramberger" piano will be a high-end instrument made in Korea; "J. Pramberger" will be a more modestly-priced instrument from Indonesia. Prices for these two new lines were not available at press time.

SMC has created a new Pramberger division within its company for distribution of Pramberger, Sohmer, and Remington pianos. Remington is a new line of low-cost pianos. Remington grands and furniture-style verticals will be made in Indonesia; other vertical models will be made for Samick in Shanghai, China.

Samick has discontinued a number of models in its Samick, Kohler & Campbell, and Conover Cable lines and has come out with some new ones as well, both Korean and Indonesian. In general, it is continuing its trend of moving most of its production to Indonesia, while concentrating its Korean production on higher-end models. At the present time, all Samick and Conover Cable brand pianos are made in Indonesia. Regular Kohler & Campbell verticals (KC models) and grands (KCG models) are made in Indonesia, while all Kohler & Campbell Millenium series verticals (KMV) and grands (KFM) are made in Korea.

Hazelton Bros. is an occasionally-used name Samick now puts on its most inexpensive Indonesian piano line. The pianos have a laminated soundboard with a basswood core surrounded by spruce veneers, a regular (rather than slow-close) fallboard on the grands, and plainer cabinetry than the company's other lines. This piano is intended to compete with the Chinese pianos of other makers.

For its higher-end pianos, Samick is now using what it calls a "Pratt Reed Premium Action." This is not to be confused with the Pratt-Read action used in many American-made pianos in the mid to late twentieth century and eventually acquired by Baldwin. Samick says its Pratt Reed action is made in Korea and designed after the German Renner action.

SAUTER

New U.S. contact:

Chris Finger Pianos
101 2nd Avenue, P.O. Box 623
Niwot, Colorado 80544

888-244-8300
303-652-3110
www.sauter-pianos.de

SCHELL, LOTHAR (new listing)

Shouda USA, Inc.
1224 Santa Anita Ave., Suite D
South El Monte, California 91733

626-350-3800
shoudausa@yahoo.com

Lothar Schell is a German piano designer whose techniques and designs have been used in pianos throughout the world. Lothar Schell vertical pianos used to be made by the Beijing Piano Co., but are now made in the company's new factory in Tieling, China, which began production in November 2003. The verticals are of Mr. Schell's own design. Features such as a variable thickness, solid spruce soundboard; off-center, full-length back posts; extra points of attachment of the action to the plate; and a number of technician-friendly features are indications of attention to detail and quality in the design of the pianos.

In 2005, Lother Schell exhibited a prototype of the first grand of his own design made at the new factory, a 6' 1" model 185. Among other things, it features a thick rim and an unusually thick beam structure. For the time being, all other Lothar Schell grands are made by the Dongbei Piano Co. and are similar to the other brands made by Dongbei.

SCHIMMEL
including Vogel

New address for U.S. distributor:

Schimmel Piano Corporation
577B Hackman Road
Lititz, Pennsylvania 17543

Schimmel has developed several new upright models based on a more traditional philosphy of construction. These are the F 122 (48"), S 125 (49"), and O 132 (52"). Older models in the same or similar sizes continue to be produced, however. In the older models, the plate is the main structural support and contains a pocket for the pinblock. In the new models, traditional back posts assume a greater role for support, and the pinblock and soundboard are attached to the posts. The company says that the joining of wooden structural and acoustical parts enhances the tone. The new models also incorporate duplex scaling.

Schimmel has created a "trilogy" of redesigned grands by marrying the front end of its 7' grand to two new grand models: a 5' 7" model 169 and a 6' 3" model 189. The company says the new models have the same treble scale and action as its 7' grand, and so have a similar sound and touch. To obtain a larger soundboard, the case sides are angled slightly, a technique now applied to all the grand models. The soundboard and ribs were also modified for tonal improvement. The 6' model 182 has been discontinued. An example of the new 5' 7" grand I played was typically bright, but had very good sustain and the feel of a larger piano.

In 2002, Schimmel acquired the PianoEurope factory in Kalisz, Poland, a piano restoration facility and manufacturer of the Meyer piano brand, one not generally found in the U.S. Schimmel is using this factory to launch its "Vogel" brand, a less expensive line named after the company's co-president. Schimmel says that although the skill level of the employees is high, lower wages and other lower costs will result in a piano approximately thirty percent less costly than the Schimmel. Vogel pianos will feature Renner actions and other parts from Schimmel or local Polish suppliers. Schimmel may gradually introduce older Schimmel scales into the Vogel pianos.

SCHUBERT

U.S. distribution of Schubert pianos from Belarus has been discontinued. At dealer request, the Schubert name is now sometimes used on inexpensive pianos from China.

SCHULZE POLLMANN

New address and phone number for U.S. distributor:

North American Music Inc.
11 Kay Fries Drive
Stony Point, New York 10980

800-782-2694

Schulze Pollmann has introduced a new 5' 3" model 160 grand. It comes with a Detoa action, but can be ordered with a Renner action at additional cost. The 46" model 117 vertical has a new scale design with agraffes and has been redesigned as model 118/P8. The 50" model 126E has been similarly redesigned and is now called 126/P6.

SEILER

New U.S. contact information for Seiler:

Seiler America
2930 Austin Bluffs Parkway, Suite 101
Colorado Springs, Colorado 80918

888-621-1137
america@seiler-pianos.com
www.seiler-pianos.com

All Seiler grand models have been redesigned with a duplex scale, longer strings, larger soundboard area, longer keys, and a lighter touch. 5' 11" model 180 has become 6' 1" model 186; 6' 9" model 206 has become 6' 10" model 208; and 8' model 240 has become 8' model 242; and there is a new 9' 1" concert grand model 278. In the Fall of 2005, Seiler will offer a new 5' 6" model 168 grand. I have had an opportunity to play models 208 and 242. Musically, both of these redesigned models are very successful. They retain the typical Seiler clarity, but with longer sustain and a marvelously even-feeling touch — a real pleasure to play.

Seiler has introduced its "Value Added Warranty." The warranty states that at the end of ten years from the date of purchase, a purchaser who has maintained his or her Seiler piano as required under the terms of the warranty may trade it in toward a new Seiler and receive a credit of the full original purchase price paid.

Seiler says that if there is no Seiler dealer in the customer's area, the customer can contact the U.S. representative to arrange for a direct purchase from Germany.

Correction: Seiler makes approximately 2,000 pianos a year.

SEJUNG (new listing)

America Sejung Corporation
295 Brea Canyon Road
Walnut, California 91789

909-839-0757
866-473-5864
sales@ASCpianos.com
www.ASCpianos.com

Pianos made by: Sejung Corp., Qingdao, China

Names used: Sejung, Falcone, Hobart M. Cable, Geo. Steck, Vivace

Sejung is a Korean-based textile, construction, and information technology business that was established in 1974, but the musical instrument portion of the business began only in 2001. In that year, the company's chairman received a proposal from an old friend with extensive experience in piano and guitar manufacturing to enter those businesses in a big way by manufacturing in China. Within a year, the company had partnered with a Chinese manufacturer (necessary for doing business in China); built a 700,000 square foot factory in Qingdao, a port city on the Eastern coast with a temperate climate; hired dozens of manufacturing managers who had once worked for Young Chang and Samick, and staffed the factory with some 2,000 workers, whom the company also feeds and houses in dormitories (necessary to attract good labor and reduce turnover). Although wages are incredibly low in China (less than one dollar per hour), the company says it has invested millions in automated production equipment in areas where precision counts, rather than just relying on cheap labor. The company produces just about every piano component in its own factories, and has a goal of producing 1,000 grand pianos and 2,000 verticals per month.

The first pianos from Sejung were shown in the U.S. in early 2003, less than one year after production began. I and other technicians examined a number of instruments at a trade show. Although still a little rough, they were definitely competent, and remarkably good for having been only an idea in someone's head less than two years earlier! Since that time, the quality has further improved. The general consensus seems to be that Sejung is destined to be a major force in the world piano market.

For marketing the pianos in the U.S., Sejung has licensed the Falcone and Geo. Steck names from PianoDisc/Mason & Hamlin and the Hobart M. Cable name from Story & Clark (see "Mason & Hamlin" and "Story & Clark" in *The Piano Book*). The names Vivace and Sejung were used briefly but have been discontinued. Initially, the pianos were sold primarily under the Falcone and Hobart M. Cable names, and the two lines were very similar. When use of the Geo. Steck name began in early 2004, the Geo. Steck and Hobart M. Cable pianos became similar (with some style differences), and the Falcone line was upgraded slightly. Specifically, most of the Falcone models have a slow-close fallboard, cast pedals and maple trapwork on the verticals, and slightly nicer cabinets. In addition, a new Falcone Georgian (FG) series includes such features as Abel hammers on grands 5' 2" and larger, upgraded soundboard material, bubinga veneer on the inside of the grand rim, real ebony sharps, and gold-colored hardware.

For model and price information, see under "Falcone," "Cable, Hobart M.," and "Steck, Geo." in the Model and Pricing Guide section of this *Supplement*.

Warranty: Twelve years on parts and ten years on labor. The warranty is not transferable.

SHERMAN CLAY

Correction: I have been told that for much of the 1970s and 1980s, pianos sold under the Sherman Clay label were made by Kimball or Aeolian. In the mid to late 1980s, some Sherman Clay pianos were made by Daewoo (Sojin).

SOHMER (& CO.)

Pianos are again being made under this venerable name, once considered among the finest of American-built instruments. However, there appears to be a dispute over the ownership of the Sohmer trademark, with pianos bearing this name being manufactured and distributed by two different companies.

SMC, distributor of Samick pianos, says it holds a license from the Burgett brothers, owners of PianoDisc, to use the Sohmer name. The Burgetts acquired the Sohmer trademark registrations when they purchased the assets of Mason & Hamlin out of bankruptcy in 1996. A distributor doing business under the name Persis International, Inc., who applied for the Sohmer trademark in 2001, claims that the registrations acquired by the Burgetts are expired and have been legally abandoned, not having been used since the 1994 closing of the Sohmer factory in Pennsylvania. The U.S. Patent and Trademark Office confirms that the government considers all past registrations of the Sohmer trademark to be expired or canceled and that the Burgetts' new application was refused. Further action on Persis' application has been temporarily suspended pending the Burgetts' appeal. At press time, the application process was still ongoing and it may be some time before the issue is settled for good. In the meantime, piano shoppers may find two "Sohmer" pianos in the marketplace. (Note: Persis' pianos are labeled "Sohmer" and SMC's are labeled "Sohmer & Co.") Both companies submitted product information, including model and price data, for this *Supplement*.

Persis International, Inc.
3540 N. Southport #116
Chicago, Illinois 60657

800-445-0695

Sohmer pianos from this distributor are manufactured by Royale, a Korean firm that is descended from the now-defunct joint venture between Ibach and Daewoo (see "Ibach"). Models include a 50" vertical and 5' 3", 5' 10", and 7' 2" grands. The pianos have high quality components, such as Renner actions, Abel hammers, Delignit pinblocks, and Ciresa soundboards.

SMC
18521 Railroad St.
City of Industry, California 91748

800-592-9393
626-964-4700
www.smcmusic.com

The Sohmer & Co. model 34, a 42" vertical, features full-length backposts, a sand-cast plate, exposed 16-ply pinblock, and a slow-close fallboard—virtually identical (except for the slow-close fallboard) to the original, highly regarded Sohmer & Co. console. A new Sohmer & Co. studio piano has a design based on the Bechstein 116 cm. scale. Production of Sohmer & Co. verticals is currently being moved from Korea to Indonesia. Sohmer & Co. grands are based on the pianos Samick made for Baldwin under the Chickering label. They have maple outer rims, sand-cast plates, spruce beams, solid brass hardware, agraffes, lacquer finishes, and other higher quality features, and are available in a variety of furntiure styles. Sohmer & Co. grands are made in Korea.

STECK, GEO.

PianoDisc has discontinued its Geo. Steck line of PianoDisc-equipped, Chinese-made pianos. The name has been licensed to new Chinese manufacturer Sejung. See "Sejung."

STEINBERG, GERH.

See "Perzina, Gebr."

STEINBERG, WILH.

New North American Agent:

Cathy Harl
Harl Pianos
318 Montgomery Street
Alexandria, Virginia 22314

703-739-2220
800-440-HARL (4275)
cathy@harlpianos.com

The name of the manufacturer has changed from Wilhelm Steinberg Pianofortefabrik Gmbh to Thüringer Pianoforte GmbH. The company has also sold its key-making business to Kluge, now part of Steinway.

Steinberg says it will not be making the 49" vertical available with a Fandrich action, as mentioned in *The Piano Book*.

The warranty has been changed to five years, parts and labor.

Although not rated in *The Piano Book*, Wilh. Steinberg pianos, both grand and vertical, are well made and would probably be rated in Group 2.

Correction: *The Piano Book* says that the Wilh. Steinberg grand is identical to the Steingraeber grand. Although the Steinberg grand evolved from the Steingraeber, unlike the Steingraeber, the Steinberg has a duplex scale, as well as a different method of rim construction and a different bridge design.

STEINER, BERNHARD

Samick is no longer making pianos under this name.

STEINGRAEBER & SÖHNE

Additional web site address: www.steingraeber.de

Steingraeber has a new 8' 11" concert grand, model E-272.

Steingraeber is known for its many innovative technical improvements to the piano. One new one is a cylindrical knuckle (grand piano part) that revolves when played softly. It acts like a normal knuckle during normal and hard playing, but the revolving knuckle makes pianissimo playing easier, smoother, and more accurate. Another is a new action for upright pianos. The "DFM" action, as it is called, contains no springs, and is now available in the model 130 vertical.

Steingraeber has entered the high-end loudspeaker manufacturing business in conjunction with a Bayreuth company.

STEINWAY & SONS

In 2005 Steinway reintroduced the legendary model A (6' 2") grand to the United States. Designed by C.F. Theodore Steinway and first offered in 1878, model A revolutionized piano making by featuring for the first time radial bracing and one-piece bent rim construction. Among other things, these features allowed the use of higher string tension and longer strings for greater volume and projection of sound. At the time the model was introduced, it was the smallest grand the company made, but was considered to provide the sound of a larger piano. Over the years, the model A has gone through several makeovers, each of slightly different size and scaling. The version being reintroduced was made from 1896 to 1914 and is the same size as the model A currently made in Steinway's plant in Hamburg, Germany.

Several years ago Steinway launched its new Legendary Collection—one-of-a-kind reproductions of historical art case pianos—with a reproduction of the famous Alma Tadema art case Steinway. Commissioned in the 1880s by Henry Marquand, then president of the Metropolitan Museum of Art in New York, this piano was designed and created by the famous English design firm of Sir Lawrence Alma-Tadema. In 1997, it was purchased at Sotheby's for $1,200,000. Offered at a price of $675,000, the reproduction, like the original, contains just about every possible art case decoration possible, including elaborate carvings, 17 different levels of decorative moldings, medallions, engravings, inlaid mother-of-pearl, marquetry, goatskin parchment, a frieze consisting of more than 6,000 parts, and even an oil painting. It is considered the most expensive piano ever built.

As mentioned in *The Piano Book*, Steinway maintains a restoration facility at its factory for the rebuilding of older Steinway pianos. Taking a cue from other firms that market "certified pre-owned" products, Steinway is now making these "Heirloom Collection Steinways" available through its dealer network. This program is designed to assist Steinway dealers in competing with rebuilders of older Steinways. The restored pianos will be identified by a medallion and will carry the same warranty as a new piano.

Steinway has made small design changes to its vertical pianos to make them easier to tune, including shortening the tuning pin length, reducing string bearing angles, correcting alignment problems in the plate, and adding string-stretching operations at the factory. Some technicians report that the vertical pianos now tune with the same ease as other brands. Steinway is also now shipping all ebony, mahogany, and walnut verticals with artist benches.

Steinway recently commemorated its 150th anniversary with numerous events, concerts, publications, and several new art case pianos. Each year brings stunning new instruments in the Art Case Collection. They can be viewed on Steinway's web site, www.steinway.com.

Correction: On page 206 of *The Piano Book*, I wrote that Steinway operated its own plate foundry until about 1930. My sources now tell me that the foundry operated until about 1939 or 1940.

STORY & CLARK

Web site address: www.storyandclark.com

In part due to economic factors and in part because of the problems of Baldwin, a principal supplier of parts, Story & Clark has ceased all its U.S. piano production. Pianos bearing the Story & Clark name are now made in China by the Dongbei piano factory, except for the upright models 120 and 140, which are made by Beijing Heintzmann. The Dongbei grands that are being outfitted with a QRS player piano system are pre-slotted and modified at the factory to accept the player system without cutting into the keys and keyframe. All pianos go to the Story & Clark facility in Pennsylvania for inspection and adjustment before being shipped to U.S. dealers.

STRAUSS

This brand improved somewhat before distribution was discontinued. The company is looking for a new U.S. distributor.

SUZUKI (new listing)

Suzuki Corporation
P.O. Box 261030
San Diego, California 92196

800-854-1594
858-566-9710
www.suzukimusic.com

Suzuki Corporation, the world's largest producer of musical instruments for education, has entered the acoustic piano business with a line of verticals and grands made in China by Dongbei. The pianos feature solid spruce soundboards, German Delignit pinblocks, and German Roslau strings.

VOGEL

See "Schimmel"

WALTER, CHARLES R.

New phone number (area code change): 574-266-0615

Web site address: www.walterpiano.com

Walter is changing over to Renner actions in its vertical pianos (they're already in the grands) and to Renner hammers on both verticals and grands. A new 5' 8" grand is scheduled for release in mid-2005.

Walter says he has made some changes to his vertical pianos to better control tuning pin torque (tightness), to reduce the incidence of false beats in the treble, and to smooth out the break between tenor and bass.

WEBER

The Weber Piano Co. described in *The Piano Book* ceased operations in 2004. The company's owner, Samsung, licensed the Weber name from Young Chang and was required by the terms of their contract to purchase all pianos bearing that name from Young Chang. In addition, it only had the rights to sell Weber pianos in North and South America. Given these restrictions, Weber found it impossible to turn a profit in a changing business environment involving the existence of numerous new Chinese companies. Samsung first tried to purchase the Weber name from Young Chang, and then to distance itself from Young Chang by starting up a "Behning" line of pianos made in China by Sejung. These efforts proved unsuccessful, however, resulting in the decision to close Weber rather than continue to lose money. Samsung will continue to honor Weber warranties through Meadowlands Piano Co. (the new name for its piano division), which continues to answer the phone number for Weber listed in *The Piano Book* (201-902-0920).

Now that Samsung's license to use the Weber name has terminated, Young Chang is planning to use it once again. See under "Young Chang" for more information.

WEINBERGER

U.S. contact:

Cathy Harl
Harl Pianos
318 Montgomery Street
Alexandria, VA 22314

703-739-2220
800-440-HARL (4275)
cathy@harlpianos.com

Pianos made by: Klavierhaus Weinberger, Brucknerstrasse 21, A 4470 Enns, Austria; phone 43-7223-86084-0, fax 43-7223-86084-20; klavierhaus@weinberger.net, www.weinberger-pianos.com

Bruno Weinberger is an Austrian piano technician who markets his own line of pianos. Distribution in the U.S. is very limited. For the most part, the pianos are manufactured by Thüringer Pianoforte GmbH, the maker of Wilh. Steinberg pianos, with Mr. Weinberger providing the musical finishing work. Mr. Weinberger says that the verticals are similar to the Wilh. Steinberg line, but that the grands are built to his own design. The grands have a couple of unique cabinet design features. The closed lid is supported on short posts so that even in the closed position there is a small space for sound to escape. The music desk folds down into the front part of the lid.

WHELPDALE, MAXWELL & CODD

This company was renamed The British Piano Manufacturing Company Ltd. See under that name for more information. The company ceased operations in April 2003.

WOODCHESTER

Woodchester was purchased by Whelpdale, Maxwell & Codd, later called The British Piano Manufacturing Company Ltd., which ceased operations in April 2003. See under "British" for more information.

WYMAN (new listing)

Wyman Piano Company
P.O. Box 218802
Nashville, Tennessee 37221

615-356-9143
george.benson@wymanpiano.com
www.wymanpiano.com

Wyman Piano Company is a new venture created by experienced former Baldwin executives. The Wyman line consists of six vertical piano sizes and four grand sizes in a variety of cabinet styles and finishes. All are manufactured in China by the Beijing Xinghai Piano Company (see "Beijing Xinghai"). Wyman says that its executives make frequent trips to Beijing to monitor manufacturing and inspect finished instruments. The pianos come with a ten-year transferable parts and labor warranty.

XINGHAI

See "Beijing Xinghai"

YAMAHA
including Disklavier

Yamaha has replaced its 4' 11" model GA1 and GA1E grands and corresponding Disklavier models with model GB1 (and Disklaviers) of the same size. The GB1 has a new scale design and some plate changes for better tuning stability.

Perhaps in response to criticisms of the tone of its 5' 3" GH1B series of grands (or perhaps because the introduction of an inexpensive piano from Indonesia has made the low-priced 5' 3" pianos redundant), Yamaha has replaced the GH1B series, and the less-expensive variant model GP1, with a new 5' 3" GC1 series. The new models feature the same scale design, duplex scaling, and tone collector construction as the more expensive C1 series, but with a bass sustain pedal instead of a sostenuto, and with less expensive

53

cabinetry and plate finish. The price of the GC1 is about the same as the GH1B and it is available in most of the same furniture styles and finishes. A Disklavier version of the GC1 replaces the corresponding Disklavier versions of the GH1B and GP1 pianos being discontinued.

The model C1 "Metro" and its Disklavier counterpart are special centennial edition pianos with a unique rim design in polished ebony and champagne gold. They mark the 100th anniversary of the first Yamaha grand.

Model M475 is a new 44" console with cabinetry sophistication halfway between models M450 and M500. Model M425 is an entry-level version of the M450 with simpler cabinetry and finish. Model P600 is a fancy furniture version of the popular P22 studio. Satin ebony versions of models P22 and T116 have been added. The polished ebony T116S is a special limited edition with silver hardware. Upright models U1 and U3 now sport a longer music desk—a very welcome addition. Model U3 joins model U5 in the use of a "floating" soundboard support system—the soundboard is not completely attached to the back at the top, allowing it to vibrate a little more freely for enhanced tonal performance.

The "A" at the end of some Disklavier model designations refers to the CD (audio) function in these instruments, one of the Mark III (i.e., third generation) Disklavier features. Disklavier grands are no longer available without the CD function. Most Disklavier verticals don't have the CD function; however, it can be added. DCD1 is an add-on CD drive that can be added to any Disklavier grand or vertical, new or old.

The model DU1A is a new Disklavier version of the 48" U1 upright. It is the only Disklavier upright with Mark III features. It replaces both the MX1Z Disklavier and the MPX1Z Disklavier with Silent Feature. The DU1A contains the Silent Feature; a version of this model without the Silent Feature is no longer offered. The 48" MIDIPiano model MP1Z will become the MPU1.

In late 2004, Yamaha released the Mark IV version of the Disklavier. It contains: an 80 gigabyte hard drive capable of holding all the Disklavier software ever written (and then some!); a tablet or pocket remote control to communicate wirelessly with the Disklavier (pocket on the GC1, C1 and C2 models, both tablet and pocket on C3 and above); built-in ethernet for connecting to your network and downloading MIDI files; the ability to play much softer as a result of a higher-speed CPU, greater MIDI resolution, and improved solenoids; more sensitive recording capabilities due to the use of greyscale (continuous) hammershank and key sensors; karaoke capability, with pitch correction when your singing is off key; an improved speaker system; and more. The performance level of the Mark IV Diskalvier is the same as formerly found in the Mark III Pro series. A limited-edition Elton John Signature model is available in several sizes of Mark IV Disklavier. Playback-only versions of models DGB1 and DGC1 will continue to use the Mark III system.

PianoSmart technology is a new feature of all Mark III and Mark IV Disklavier pianos. Yamaha has prepared a piano track in MIDI format on a floppy disk to go along with each of a number of popular audio CDs available on the general market. When the owner plays both the floppy and the CD at the same time, PianoSmart links them together, enabling the Disklavier to accurately play along with the CD. One can also record a piano accompaniment to a favorite audio CD. Pop the CD and a blank floppy into a Mark III or Mark IV Disklavier and record yourself playing along. The two will then be linked together for future playback. PianoSmart is available as a free software upgrade from Yamaha. The "smart" MIDI files will be added to the library of Disklavier musical offerings available from Yamaha. Customers with older Disklavier versions can retrofit PianoSmart into their system by buying the DCD1 Disklavier CD player and a software upgrade, although it may require a memory upgrade as well.

To help its dealers overcome competition from "grey market" pianos, Yamaha has begun an "Heirloom Assurance" program that provides a five-year warranty on a used Yamaha piano less than twenty-five years old purchased from an authorized Yamaha dealer. Obviously, the instrument must be a Yamaha originally manufactured for the U.S. market. For the piano to be eligible for the warranty, the dealer must first submit technical information about the piano's condition to Yamaha and gain the company's approval.

YOUNG CHANG
including Bergmann, Pramberger, and Weber

New U.S. distributor information:

AND Music Corporation
10107 S. Tacoma Way A-3
Lakewood, Washington 98499

253-589-3580

Young Chang America has changed its corporate name to AND Music Corporation.

In *The Piano Book*, it was stated that Young Chang was retiring its "Gold" series in favor of its Pramberger Signature series. The Gold series has now been resurrected as Young Chang's upper-level Chinese line from its factory in Tianjin, China. Model numbers begin with "G." It differs from the company's Bergmann line (also made in China) as follows: Warranty (twelve years on Young Chang Gold, ten years on Bergmann); cosmetic differences in legs, casters, plate color, inner rim color, lid, other cabinetry; tapered soundboard and upgraded hammers on Young Chang Gold grands; laminated soundboard on Bergmann verticals, solid spruce soundboard on Young Chang Gold verticals.

All Bergmann model numbers now begin with "B," the grands with "BTG." A new 5' 9" model BTG-175 and 6' 1" model BTG-185, both made in China, are based on the scales of the corresponding Young Chang Gold series pianos.

Young Chang says it has changed the front duplex scale on all its grand models to a new configuration for a cleaner sound.

In March 2004, Young Chang's Korean rival, Samick, acquired a controlling interest in Young Chang. Under Samick's control, the company then entered into an agreement with Samick's U.S. distributor, SMC, to handle all U.S. distribution and administration of Young Chang products from SMC headquarters in the Los Angeles area. The existing inventory of Young Chang pianos and piano parts held by AND Music Corporation (Young Chang America) was controlled by SMC as well.

In September 2004, however, the Korean Fair Trade Commission ruled that Samick's purchase of Young Chang violated Korean anti-monopoly laws and ordered Samick to sell its interest in Young Chang within a year, an order Samick is contesting. Naturally, Samick stopped making payments to creditors on Young Chang's behalf, forcing Young Chang into bankruptcy. In December 2005, the court-appointed receiver for the Korean bankruptcy court cancelled the SMC/Young Chang distribution agreement and reconstituted AND Music Corporation as the exclusive U.S. distributor for Young Chang products. For a time, both SMC and AND were claiming to be the "real" Young Chang distributor, both providing Young Chang and Bergmann pianos to dealers. In March 2005, a U.S. court ruled that the inventory SMC had taken from AND should be returned, at least temporarily ending SMC's distribution of these products, pending further litigation. Both companies have said they will honor the warranty of any pianos they supplied to dealers. Young Chang says it has received an influx of new capital and is in the process of reorganizing the company. Until Young Chang is discharged from bankruptcy, consumers are advised that for additional security they may wish to ask the dealer to supplement the factory warranty with a written warranty from the dealer.

Concerning Young Chang's Pramberger line of pianos, Pramberger was a name used by Young Chang under license from piano engineer Joseph Pramberger. When Mr. Pramberger died in 2003, his estate had the opportunity to terminate its relationship with Young Chang and did so. Samick quickly licensed the rights to the Pramberger name. However, Young Chang still holds the rights to the original designs, and will be making them under different names. The Young Chang Pramberger Signature series (P) has been renamed the Young Chang Premier (P) series. The Pramberger Platinum (JP) series has been renamed the Young Chang Platinum (YP) series. The name on the fallboard will read "Young Chang" instead of "Pramberger."

Prior to the name change, Young Chang had added a 52" vertical and 7' 6" grand to the Pramberger Platinum line. Beginning in 2003, all Pramberger Platinum grands came with a Pramberger/Renner action (Renner parts on a Pramberger action frame), including the damper action. These actions can be identified by their wooden action rail and the Renner label. Please see under "Samick" for more information on Pramberger pianos.

Following the demise of the Samsung-owned Weber Piano Co. (see "Weber"), Young Chang took back the Weber name, which it owns, and says it plans to bring out a line of Weber pianos patterned after existing Young Chang and Bergmann pianos and the former Pramberger line. The Weber "Legend" series will be like the Bergmann, "Dynasty" like Young Chang Gold, "Sovereign" like the Young Chang Premier series (formerly Pramberger Signature), and "Albert Weber" like Young Chang Platinum (formerly Pramberger Platinum).

The Kurzweil Player System (KPS) is similar to the QRS Ancho system when installed in Young Chang pianos. When installed in Bergmann pianos, the KPS is only available as the QRS 2000 CD+ system.

OTHER ITEMS OF INTEREST

MOOG PIANO BAR

Moog Music Inc.
554C Riverside Drive
Asheville, North Carolina 28801

828-251-0090
info@moogmusic.com
www.moogmusic.com

Moog Music Inc., founded by electronic music pioneer Robert Moog, has introduced an amazingly simple and elegant way of turning any acoustic piano into a MIDI controller without modifying the piano in any way. The system consists of three parts: A *scanner bar* sits on the cheek blocks, spanning the keyboard immediately in front of the fallboard and slightly above the keys. Optical sensors in the scanner bar measure the movement of the keys and translate it into note and velocity information. A *pedal sensor* rests beneath the pedals and detects their motion. A *control module* sits on the piano, receiving the data from the scanner bar and pedal sensor, turning it into MIDI information that can trigger over 300 built-in sounds. The control module can hold up to 100 setups, twenty of which can be stored on a portable "library card," twenty that are factory-supplied, and sixty that are user-determined. The control module also contains a headphone jack, audio outputs, and MIDI in and out ports. The Moog Piano Bar is completely portable and comes with a carrying case. It sells for about $1,495 from piano dealers, selected piano technicians, and musical instrument dealers.

MODEL and PRICING GUIDE

This guide contains the "list price" for nearly every brand, model, style, and finish of new piano that has regular distribution in the United States and, for the most part, Canada. Some marginal, local, or "stencil" brands are omitted. Except where indicated, prices are in U.S. dollars and the pianos are assumed to be for sale in the U.S. (Canadians will find the information useful after translation into Canadian dollars, but there may be differences in import duties and sales practices that will affect retail prices.) Prices and specifications are, of course, subject to change. Most manufacturers revise their prices at least once a year; two or three times a year is not uncommon when currency exchange rates are unstable. The prices in this edition were compiled in the spring of 2005.

Note that prices of most European pianos vary with the value of the dollar against the Euro. For this *Supplement*, the exchange rate used was Euro = $1.30. All prices are "landed" prices, i.e., including import duties and estimated costs of freight to the U.S. warehouse or port of entry. However, such costs will vary depending on the shipping method employed, the port of entry, and other variables.

Some terms used in this guide require special explanation and disclaimers:

List Price

The list price is usually a starting point for negotiation, not a final sales price. The term "list price," as used in this *Supplement*, is a "standard" or "normalized" list price computed from the published wholesale price according to a formula commonly used in the industry. Some manufacturers use a different formula, however, for their own suggested retail prices, usually one that raises the prices above "standard" list by ten to fifty percent so that their dealers can advertise a larger "discount" without losing profit. For this reason, price-shopping by comparing discounts from the manufacturers' own suggested retail prices may result in a faulty price comparison. To provide a level playing field for comparing prices, all prices in this guide are computed according to a uniform "standard" formula, *even though it may differ from the manufacturers' own suggested retail prices.* Where my list prices and those of a manufacturer differ, then, no dishonesty should be inferred; we simply employ different formulas. For most brands, but not all, the price includes a bench and the standard manufacturer's warranty for that brand (see *The Piano Book* for details). Prices for some European brands do not include a bench. Most dealers will also include moving and one or two tunings in the home, but these are optional and a matter of agreement between you and the dealer.

Style and Finish

Unless otherwise indicated, the cabinet style is assumed to be "traditional" and is not stated. Exactly what "traditional" means varies from brand to brand. In general, it is a "classic" styling with minimal embellishment and straight legs. The vertical pianos have front legs, which are free-standing on smaller verticals and attached to the cabinet with toe blocks on larger verticals. "Continental" or European styling refers to vertical pianos without decorative trim and usually without front legs. Other furniture styles (Chippendale, French Provincial, Queen Anne, etc.) are as noted. The manufacturer's own trademarked style name is used when an appropriate generic name could not be determined.

Unless otherwise stated, all finishes are assumed to be "satin," which reflects light but not images. "Polished" finishes, also known as "high-gloss" or "high-polish," are mirror-like. "Oiled" finishes are usually matte (not shiny). "Open-pore" finishes, common on some European pianos, are slightly grainier satin finishes due to the wood pores not being filled in prior to finishing. In fact, many finishes labeled "satin" on European pianos are actually open-pore. "Ebony" is a black finish.

Special-order–only styles and finishes are in italics.

Some descriptions of style and finish may be slightly different from the manufacturer's own for the purpose of clarity, consistency, saving space, or other reason.

Size

The height of a vertical piano is measured from the floor to the top of the piano. The length of a grand piano is measured from the very front (keyboard end) to the very back (tail end).

About Actual Selling or "Street" Prices

Buying a piano is something like buying a car—the list price is deliberately set high in anticipation of negotiating.[*] But sometimes this is carried to extremes, as when the salesperson reduces the price three times in the first fifteen minutes to barely half the sticker price. In situations like this, the customer, understandably confused, is bound to ask in exasperation, "What is the *real* price of this piano?"

Unfortunately, there *is* no "real" price. In theory, the dealer pays a wholesale price and then marks it up by an amount sufficient to cover the overhead and produce a profit. In practice, however, the markup can vary considerably from sale to sale depending on such factors as:

- how long the inventory has been sitting around, racking up finance charges for the dealer

- how much of a discount the dealer received at the wholesale level for buying in quantity or for paying cash

- the dealer's cash flow situation

- the competition in that particular geographic area for a particular brand or type of piano

- special piano sales events taking place in the area

- how the salesperson sizes up your situation and your willingness to pay

- the level of pre- and post-sale service the dealer seeks to provide

- the dealer's other overhead expenses

It's not unusual for one person to pay fifty percent more than another for the same brand and model of piano—sometimes even from the same dealer on the same day! It may seem as if pricing is so chaotic that no advice can be given, but in truth, enough piano sales do fall within a certain range of typical profit margins that some guidance is possible as long as the reader understands the limitations inherent in this kind of advice.

Historically, discounts from "standard" list price have averaged ten or fifteen percent in the piano business. In recent years, however, conditions

---

[*] A relatively small number of dealers have non-negotiable prices.

have changed such that, according to some industry sources, the average discount from list has increased to twenty or twenty-five percent. Essentially, due to growing competition from used pianos and digital pianos, and a decrease in the cultural importance attached to having a piano in the home, there are too many dealers of new pianos chasing after too few consumer dollars. In addition, higher labor costs in some parts of the world and unfavorable international currency values make some brands so expensive in the U.S. that they can only be sold at very large discounts. I think, too, that consumers are becoming more savvy and are shopping around. Unfortunately, the overhead costs of running a traditional piano store are so high that most dealers cannot stay in business if they sell at an average discount from "standard" list price of more than about twenty percent. To survive, dealers are evolving multiple new approaches: becoming more efficient, instituting low-price/high volume strategies, cutting their overhead—sometimes including service—or subsidizing their meager sales of new pianos with used pianos (which command higher profit margins), rentals, rebuilding, and other products and services.

Although the average discount has increased, it is by no means uniform. Some brands dependably bring top dollar; others languish or the price is highly situational. I did consider giving a typical range of "street" prices for each brand and model listed in this volume, but concluded that the task would be too daunting due to the extreme variation that can exist from one situation to another, and because of the political fallout that would likely result from dealers and manufacturers who fear the loss of what little power they still have over aggressive, price-shopping customers. So, for now, I've decided just to give general advice in print. (For those who desire more specific information on "street" prices, I offer additional services, such as private telephone consultations and a Pricing Guide Service on the internet. See my web site, **www.pianobook.com**, for more information.)

One way some manufacturers assist dealers in overcoming downward price pressure is to publish wholesale price lists that are less than honest. That is, dealers are routinely offered large discounts (ten to thirty percent) from the published wholesale price if they buy in sufficient quantity, or for certain models, or for any other reason the manufacturer can think of. Since the prices in this *Supplement* are calculated from the published wholesale prices, this practice results in over-inflated list prices in this book for those particular companies, allowing dealers of those brands to advertise larger "discounts" without losing profit. This practice is especially common among some Chinese and Korean companies, but seems to be spreading. (Most manufacturers offer small discounts from the published wholesale price list from time to time or for paying cash, but lately some manufacturers seem to be carrying this practice to greater heights.) The problem for the consumer is that these wholesale discounts are not given out uniformly by manufacturers or among dealers, another reason why an appropriate "street" price figured from the price information presented here will have to remain a rough estimate.

It should be clearly understood that the advice given here is based on my own observations, subjective judgment, and general understanding of the piano market, *not* on statistical sales data or scientific analysis. (Brand-by-brand statistical sales data are virtually nonexistent.) This knowledge is the product of discussions with hundreds of customers, dealers, technicians, and industry executives over the years. Other industry observers may come to different conclusions. This rundown of "street" prices won't cover every brand, but should give a rough idea of what to expect and the ability to predict prices for some of the brands not specifically covered. I can't emphasize enough, however, that pricing can be highly situational, dependent on the mix of available products and the ease of comparison shopping in any particular geographic area, as well as on the financial situation of dealer and customer. The following generalizations should prove useful to you, but expect almost anything.

As a general rule of thumb:

- the more expensive the piano, the higher the possible discount

- the more "exclusive" a brand is perceived to be, the less likely head-to-head competition, and therefore the lower the possible discount

- the longer a piano remains unsold, the higher the possible discount

- the more service-intensive the piano, the lower the possible discount

Although discounts from "standard" list price for most Japanese and Korean pianos typically start at perhaps fifteen percent, twenty or even thirty percent discounts are not uncommon in a moderately competitive environment, especially if the dealer knows the customer is shopping around. Chinese and Indonesian pianos, on the other hand, are so inexpensive, and some still require so much servicing by the dealer, that it's simply not cost-effective to sell them for much less than full list price. Expect little or no discount. Some dealers just use them as "loss leaders," that is, just to get people into the store, whereupon the customer is sold on a more expensive piano.

The Boston piano, although manufactured in Asia, is generally viewed as being a little more "exclusive" due to its association with Steinway, so deep discounting is much less likely. Discounts in the range of ten percent or so are common. Baldwin, whose pianos are usually seen as being distinctly different from the Asian products even though they often share common price ranges, also benefits from exceptional name recognition and its historical "made in USA" connection. Discounting is likely to be moderate, in my experience—perhaps fifteen to twenty-five percent. (Note: Due to Baldwin's recent bankruptcy and sale, however, discounting has tended to be larger than usual during the past couple of years. Until this situation settles down, some very large discounts may be possible on Baldwin products in selected situations.)

Western European instruments tend to be extremely expensive here due to their high quality, the high European cost of doing business, additional middlemen/importers and, recently, unfavorable exchange rates. There appear to be two types of dealers of these pianos. One type, specializing in selling higher-quality instruments to a demanding clientele, manages to get top dollar for them despite their high price, with discounts averaging only twenty percent or so. They are not particularly into negotiating. The other type of dealer, probably more numerous, depends for his or her "bread and butter" on consumer-grade pianos and is pleased to make a relatively small profit on the occasional sale of a luxury instrument. Discounts here may well approach thirty to forty percent at times, especially if the piano has gone unsold for an extended period of time. Eastern European brands like Petrof and Estonia are already seen as being a good deal for the money, so expect moderate discounts—perhaps fifteen to twenty-five percent.

Steinway pianos have always been in a class by themselves, historically the only expensive piano to continually command high profit margins. Except for older Steinways and the occasional Mason & Hamlin, Steinway has little competition and fewer than one hundred dealers in the United States. Service requirements can be quite high, at least in part because of the higher standards often required to satisfy a fussier clientele. Historically, Steinway pianos have sold at or near full list price. (Some dealers even sell *above* list!) This is still true in many places, but in recent years I have seen a little more discounting than in the past. Ten to fifteen percent is not unusual in some areas; as much as twenty percent would be rare.

For brands not mentioned or implied in the above discussion, it's usually a safe bet to figure a discount of fifteen to twenty-five percent from the prices in this *Supplement*, with greater discounts possible in selected situations.

There is no "fair" price for a piano except the one the buyer and seller agree on. The dealer is no more obligated to sell you a piano at a deep discount than you are obligated to pay the list price. Many dealers are simply not able to sell at the low end of the range consistently and still stay in business. It's understandable that you would like to pay the lowest price possible, and there's no harm in asking, but remember that piano shopping is not just about chasing the lowest price. Be sure you are getting the instrument that best suits your needs and preferences and that the dealer is committed to providing the proper pre- and post-sale service.

(Note: Remember that the "street" price discounts suggested above should be subtracted from the "standard" list prices in this *Supplement*, not from the manufacturer's suggested retail price.)

For more information on shopping for a new piano and on how to save money, please see pages 60–75 in *The Piano Book* (fourth edition).

Astin-Weight

Verticals

Model	Size	Style and Finish	Price
U-500	50"	Oiled Oak	13,380.
U-500	50"	Santa Fe Oiled Oak	14,780.
U-500	50"	Lacquer Oak	13,780.
U-500	50"	Oiled Walnut	13,980.
U-500	50"	Lacquer Walnut	14,380.

Grands

Model	Size	Style and Finish	Price
———	5' 9"	Ebony	35,700.

August Förster — see "Förster, August"

Baldwin

Verticals

Model	Size	Style and Finish	Price
660E	43-1/2"	Georgian Mahogany	6,890.
662E	43-1/2"	Queen Anne Regency Cherry	6,890.
665E	43-1/2"	Transitional Country Oak	6,890.
667E	43-1/2"	Country French Oak	5,776.
2090E	43-1/2"	Hepplewhite Vintage Mahogany	8,020.
2095E	43-1/2"	Regal Oak	6,176.
2096E	43-1/2"	Queen Anne Royal Cherry	8,020.
243E	45"	Ebony	8,360.
243E	45"	Golden Oak	8,360.
243E	45"	American Walnut	8,360.
243E	45"	Lyptus Wood Clear Finish	8,360.
243Elvis	45"	Elvis Presley Signature	11,334.
GSV10	45"	Gibson Les Paul	16,360.
5050E	45"	Mahogany	11,230.
5052E	45"	Limited Edition Queen Anne Cherry	11,230.
5057E	45"	Limited Edition Georgian Oak	11,230.
5062E	45"	Queen Anne Distressed Cherry	11,890.
248E	48"	American Walnut	11,990.
6000E	52"	Ebony	15,620.
6000E	52"	Mahogany	15,620.
6000E	52"	Regency Cherry with Gold Trim	17,150.

Model	Size	Style and Finish	Price*

Grands

Model	Size	Style and Finish	Price*
M1	5' 2"	Ebony and Polished Ebony	41,340.
M1	5' 2"	Mahogany/Walnut	42,540.
M1	5' 2"	Polished Mahogany/Walnut/Cherry	45,140.
225E	5' 2"	French Provincial Cherry	50,940.
R1	5' 8"	Ebony and Polished Ebony	46,540.
R1	5' 8"	Mahogany/Walnut	48,214.
R1	5' 8"	Polished Mahogany/Walnut	51,030.
226E	5' 8"	French Provincial Cherry and Pol. Cherry	56,840.
227E	5' 8"	Louis XVI Mahogany	56,840.
L1	6' 3"	Ebony and Polished Ebony	52,460.
L1	6' 3"	Mahogany/Walnut	54,420.
L1	6' 3"	Polished Mahogany/Walnut/Cherry	57,480.
SF10E	7'	Ebony	73,580.
SF10E	7'	Polished Ebony	74,760.
SD10	9'	Ebony	115,780.
SD10	9'	Polished Ebony	123,900.

ConcertMaster (approximate, including installation by factory or dealer)

Grands		Playback only / with Perf. Option	7,024./8,058.
		With stop rail, add $314	

Note: Discounts may apply, especially as an incentive to purchase the piano.

Baldwin, D.H.

Verticals

Model	Size	Style and Finish	Price*
561	43-1/2"	Lyptus Wood Clear Finish	3,998.
562	43-1/2"	Red Cherry/Brown Cherry	3,998.
562	43-1/2"	Distressed Red Cherry/Brown Cherry	3,998.
569	43-1/2"	Lyptus Wood Ebony	3,998.
570	43-1/2"	Lyptus Wood Mahogany	5,338.
572	43-1/2"	Red Cherry	5,338.

Bechstein, (C.)

Models beginning with "A" say only "Bechstein" on the fallboard. Others say "C. Bechstein." See article in Manufacturer and Product Update section of this Supplement for details.

*For explanation of terms and prices, please see pages 59–65.

Bechstein, (C.) (continued)

Bechstein Verticals

Model	Size	Style and Finish	Price
A-3	45-1/2"	Polished Ebony	15,780.
A-3	45-1/2"	Mahogany/Walnut/Cherry/Alder	15,160.
A-3	45-1/2"	Polished Mahogany/Walnut/Cherry	16,800.
A-3	45-1/2"	Polished White	16,600.
A-2	47"	Polished Ebony	17,200.
A-2	47"	Mahogany/Walnut/Cherry	17,000.
A-2	47"	Polished Mahogany/Walnut/Cherry	18,200.
A-2	47"	Polished White	18,000.
A-2	47"	Polished Blue	18,800.
A-1	49"	Polished Ebony	18,400.
A-1	49"	Mahogany/Walnut/Cherry	18,200.
A-1	49"	Polished Mahogany/Walnut/Cherry	19,800.
A-1	49"	Polished White	19,800.

C. Bechstein Verticals

Model	Size	Style and Finish	Price
Balance	45-1/2"	Polished Ebony	33,600.
Avance	46-1/2"	Polished Ebony	37,800.
Ars Nova	49"	Polished Ebony	35,000.
Concert 8	51-1/2"	Polished Ebony	46.800.
Concert 8	51-1/2"	Mahogany/Walnut/Cherry	46,800.
Concert 8	51-1/2"	Polished Mahogany/Walnut/Cherry	48,800.
Concert 8	51-1/2"	Polished White	48,800.

Bechstein Grands

Model	Size	Style and Finish	Price
A-160	5' 3"	Polished Ebony	48,600.
A-160	5' 3"	Polished Mahogany	50,400.
A-160	5' 3"	Polished White	52,400.
A-160	5' 3"	Special Woods	52,400.
A-190	6' 3"	Polished Ebony	51,900.
A-190	6' 3"	Polished Mahogany	53,700.
A-190	6' 3"	Polished White	55,600.
A-208	6' 9"	Ebony and Polished Ebony	56,000.
A-208	6' 9"	Polished Mahogany	57,400.
A-208	6' 9"	Polished White	57,400.

C. Bechstein Grands

Model	Size	Style and Finish	Price
M/P 192	6' 4"	Ebony and Polished Ebony	97,000.
M/P 192	6' 4"	Mahogany/Walnut/Cherry	98,000.
M/P 192	6' 4"	Polished Mahogany/Walnut/Cherry	102,000.
M/P 192	6' 4"	Polished White	102,000.

Model	Size	Style and Finish	Price*
M/P 192	6' 4"	Special Woods	120,000.
B-210	6' 11"	Ebony and Polished Ebony	114,000.
C-232	7' 7"	Polished Ebony	139,000.
D-280	9' 2"	Polished Ebony	184,400.

Bergmann

Verticals

BE-109	43"	Continental Polished Ebony	2,900.
BE-109	43"	Continental Polished Mahogany	2,990.
BE-109	43"	Continental Polished Ivory	2,900.
BAF-108	43"	Mahogany	3,390.
BAF-108	43"	Queen Anne Oak/Cherry	3,390.
BAF-108	43"	Mediterranean Oak	3,390.
BAF-108	43"	French Provincial Cherry	3,390.
BAF-108	43"	Italian Walnut	3,390.
BE-118	47"	Polished Ebony	3,800.
BE-118	47"	Polished Mahogany	3,900.
BAF-118	47"	Cherry	3,580.
BE-120C	47"	Polished Mahogany	3,840.
BE-120CD	47"	Polished Mahogany	3,900.
BE-121	48"	Polished Ebony	3,560.
BE-121	48"	Polished Mahogany/Walnut/Bubinga	3,680.
BE-131	52"	Polished Ebony	3,770.
BE-131	52"	Polished Mahogany/Walnut/Bubinga	3,890.

Grands

BTG-150	4' 11"	Polished Ebony	8,810.
BTG-150	4' 11"	Polished Mahogany	9,010.
BTG-150	4' 11"	Polished Ivory	8,810.
BTG-157	5' 2"	Polished Ebony	9,860.
BTG-157	5' 2"	Polished Mahogany	9,980.
BTG-157	5' 2"	Polished Ivory	9,860.
BTG-175	5' 9"	Polished Ebony	11,120.
BTG-175	5' 9"	Polished Mahogany	11,320.
BTG-185	6' 1"	Polished Ebony	11,960.
BTG-185	6' 1"	Polished Mahogany	12,300.

*For explanation of terms and prices, please see pages 59–65.

Blüthner

Prices do not include bench.

Verticals

Model	Size	Style and Finish	Price*
I	45"	Ebony and Polished Ebony	22,531.
I	45"	Walnut and Polished Walnut	23,543.
I	45"	Mahogany and Polished Mahogany	23,420.
I	45"	Cherry and Polished Cherry	23,420.
I	45"	White and Polished White	23,543.
C	46"	Ebony and Polished Ebony	23,786.
C	46"	Walnut and Polished Walnut	25,011.
C	46"	Mahogany and Polished Mahogany	24,772.
C	46"	Cherry and Polished Cherry	24,891.
C	46"	White and Polished White	25,011.
C	46"	Polished Bubinga/Yew/Macassar Ebony	26,202.
C	46"	Saxony Polished Pyramid Mahogany	31,426.
C	46"	Saxony Polished Burl Walnut Inlay	31,728.
A	49"	Ebony and Polished Ebony	30,338.
A	49"	Walnut and Polished Walnut	31,853.
A	49"	Mahogany and Polished Mahogany	31,549.
A	49"	Cherry and Polished Cherry	31,703.
A	49"	White and Polished White	31,853.
A	49"	Polished Bubinga/Yew/Macassar Ebony	33,372.
A	49"	Saxony Polished Pyramid Mahogany	40,026.
A	49"	Saxony Polished Burl Walnut Inlay	40,412.
B	52"	Ebony and Polished Ebony	34,638.
B	52"	Walnut and Polished Walnut	36,369.
B	52"	Mahogany and Polished Mahogany	36,023.
B	52"	Cherry and Polished Cherry	36,194.
B	52"	White and Polished White	36,369.
B	52"	Polished Bubinga/Yew/Macassar Ebony	38,100.
B	52"	Saxony Polished Pyramid Mahogany	45,700.
B	52"	Saxony Polished Burl Walnut Inlay	46,140.
—	—	*Sostenuto pedal on vertical piano, add'l*	2,160.

Grands

Model	Size	Style and Finish	Price*
11	5' 1"	Ebony and Polished Ebony	61,424.
11	5' 1"	Walnut and Polished Walnut	64,496.
11	5' 1"	Mahogany and Polished Mahogany	63,881.
11	5' 1"	Cherry and Polished Cherry	64,189.
11	5' 1"	White and Polished White	64,496.

Model	Size	Style and Finish	Price*
11	5' 1"	Polished Bubinga/Yew/Macassar Ebony	67,569.
11	5' 1"	Saxony Polished Pyramid Mahogany	81,045.
11	5' 1"	Saxony Polished Burl Walnut Inlay	81,823.
11	5' 1"	"President" Polished Ebony	68,577.
11	5' 1"	"President" Polished Mahogany	71,320.
11	5' 1"	"President" Polished Walnut	72,004.
11	5' 1"	"President" Polished Bubinga	75,434.
11	5' 1"	Louis XV Ebony and Polished Ebony	71,692.
11	5' 1"	Louis XV Mahogany and Pol. Mahogany	75,278.
11	5' 1"	Louis XV Walnut and Polished Walnut	74,559.
11	5' 1"	"Kaiser Wilhelm II" Polished Ebony	72,316.
11	5' 1"	"Kaiser Wilhelm II" Polished Mahogany	75,209.
11	5' 1"	"Kaiser Wilhelm II" Polished Walnut	75,931.
11	5' 1"	"Kaiser Wilhelm II" Polished Cherry	75,570.
11	5' 1"	"Ambassador" East Indian Rosewood	84,160.
11	5' 1"	"Ambassador" Walnut	77,927.
11	5' 1"	"Nicolas II" Walnut with Burl Inlay	84,160.
11	5' 1"	Louis XVI Rococo White with Gold	90,396.
11	5' 1"	"Classic Alexandra" Polished Ebony	69,824.
11	5' 1"	"Classic Alexandra" Polished Mahogany	73,313.
11	5' 1"	"Classic Alexandra" Polished Walnut	72,615.
10	5' 5"	Ebony and Polished Ebony	70,808.
10	5' 5"	Walnut and Polished Walnut	74,349.
10	5' 5"	Mahogany and Polished Mahogany	73,641.
10	5' 5"	Cherry and Polished Cherry	73,997.
10	5' 5"	White and Polished White	74,349.
10	5' 5"	Polished Bubinga/Yew/Macassar Ebony	77,890.
10	5' 5"	Saxony Polished Pyramid Mahogany	93,427.
10	5' 5"	Saxony Polished Burl Walnut Inlay	94,323.
10	5' 5"	"President" Polished Ebony	79,052.
10	5' 5"	"President" Polished Mahogany	82,215.
10	5' 5"	"President" Polished Walnut	83,004.
10	5' 5"	"President" Polished Bubinga	86,958.
10	5' 5"	"Senator" French Walnut with Leather	86,240.
10	5' 5"	"Senator" Jacaranda Rosewd w/Leather	91,989.
10	5' 5"	Louis XV Ebony and Polished Ebony	82,646.
10	5' 5"	Louis XV Mahogany and Pol. Mahogany	86,778.
10	5' 5"	Louis XV Walnut and Polished Walnut	85,951.
10	5' 5"	"Kaiser Wilhelm II" Polished Ebony	83,365.
10	5' 5"	"Kaiser Wilhelm II" Polished Mahogany	86,698.
10	5' 5"	"Kaiser Wilhelm II" Polished Walnut	87,531.

*For explanation of terms and prices, please see pages 59–65.

Model	Size	Style and Finish	Price*

Blüthner (continued)

10	5' 5"	"Kaiser Wilhelm II" Polished Cherry	87,114.
10	5' 5"	"Ambassador" East Indian Rosewood	97,017.
10	5' 5"	"Ambassador" Walnut	89,833.
10	5' 5"	"Nicolas II" Walnut with Burl Inlay	97,017.
10	5' 5"	Louis XVI Rococo White with Gold	104,204.
10	5' 5"	"Classic Alexandra" Polished Ebony	80,490.
10	5' 5"	"Classic Alexandra" Polished Mahogany	84,514.
10	5' 5"	"Classic Alexandra" Polished Walnut	83,708.
6	6' 3"	Ebony and Polished Ebony	77,230.
6	6' 3"	Walnut and Polished Walnut	81,092.
6	6' 3"	Mahogany and Polished Mahogany	80,319.
6	6' 3"	Cherry and Polished Cherry	80,705.
6	6' 3"	White and Polished White	81,092.
6	6' 3"	Polished Bubinga/Yew/Macassar Ebony	84,954.
6	6' 3"	Saxony Polished Pyramid Mahogany	101,899.
6	6' 3"	Saxony Polished Burl Walnut Inlay	102,878.
6	6' 3"	"President" Polished Ebony	86,222.
6	6' 3"	"President" Polished Mahogany	89,670.
6	6' 3"	"President" Polished Walnut	90,531.
6	6' 3"	"President" Polished Bubinga	94,843.
6	6' 3"	"Senator" French Walnut with Leather	94,059.
6	6' 3"	"Senator" Jacaranda Rosewd w/Leather	100,329.
6	6' 3"	Louis XV Ebony and Polished Ebony	90,139.
6	6' 3"	Louis XV Mahogany and Pol. Mahogany	94,645.
6	6' 3"	Louis XV Walnut and Polished Walnut	93,746.
6	6' 3"	"Kaiser Wilhelm II" Polished Ebony	90,923.
6	6' 3"	"Kaiser Wilhelm II" Polished Mahogany	94,559.
6	6' 3"	"Kaiser Wilhelm II" Polished Walnut	95,468.
6	6' 3"	"Kaiser Wilhelm II" Polished Cherry	95,013.
6	6' 3"	"Ambassador" East Indian Rosewood	105,815.
6	6' 3"	"Ambassador" Walnut	97,979.
6	6' 3"	"Nicolas II" Walnut with Burl Inlay	105,815.
6	6' 3"	Louis XVI Rococo White with Gold	113,655.
6	6' 3"	"Classic Alexandra" Polished Ebony	87,788.
6	6' 3"	"Classic Alexandra" Polished Mahogany	92,177.
6	6' 3"	"Classic Alexandra" Polished Walnut	91,298.
6	6' 3"	*Jubilee Edition Plate, add'l*	5,980.
4	6' 10"	Ebony and Polished Ebony	91,598.
4	6' 10"	Walnut and Polished Walnut	96,179.

Model	Size	Style and Finish	Price*
4	6' 10"	Mahogany and Polished Mahogany	95,262.
4	6' 10"	Cherry and Polished Cherry	95,720.
4	6' 10"	White and Polished White	96,179.
4	6' 10"	Polished Bubinga/Yew/Macassar Ebony	100,759.
4	6' 10"	Saxony Polished Pyramid Mahogany	120,856.
4	6' 10"	Saxony Polished Burl Walnut Inlay	122,016.
4	6' 10"	"President" Polished Ebony	102,263.
4	6' 10"	"President" Polished Mahogany	106,353.
4	6' 10"	"President" Polished Walnut	107,374.
4	6' 10"	"President" Polished Bubinga	112,488.
4	6' 10"	"Kaiser Wilhelm II" Polished Ebony	107,839.
4	6' 10"	"Kaiser Wilhelm II" Polished Mahogany	112,152.
4	6' 10"	"Kaiser Wilhelm II" Polished Walnut	113,231.
4	6' 10"	"Kaiser Wilhelm II" Polished Cherry	112,693.
4	6' 10"	"Ambassador" East Indian Rosewood	125,502.
4	6' 10"	"Ambassador" Walnut	116,207.
4	6' 10"	"Classic Alexandra" Polished Ebony	104,121.
4	6' 10"	"Classic Alexandra" Polished Mahogany	109,325.
4	6' 10"	"Classic Alexandra" Polished Walnut	108,287.
2	7' 8"	Ebony and Polished Ebony	102,374.
2	7' 8"	Walnut and Polished Walnut	107,492.
2	7' 8"	Mahogany and Polished Mahogany	106,469.
2	7' 8"	Cherry and Polished Cherry	106,982.
2	7' 8"	White and Polished White	107,492.
2	7' 8"	Polished Bubinga/Yew/Macassar Ebony	112,613.
2	7' 8"	Saxony Polished Pyramid Mahogany	135,074.
2	7' 8"	Saxony Polished Burl Walnut Inlay	136,373.
2	7' 8"	"President" Polished Ebony	114,294.
2	7' 8"	"President" Polished Mahogany	118,863.
2	7' 8"	"President" Polished Walnut	120,006.
2	7' 8"	"President" Polished Bubinga	125,721.
2	7' 8"	"Kaiser Wilhelm II" Polished Ebony	120,526.
2	7' 8"	"Kaiser Wilhelm II" Polished Mahogany	125,349.
2	7' 8"	"Kaiser Wilhelm II" Polished Walnut	126,554.
2	7' 8"	"Kaiser Wilhelm II" Polished Cherry	125,950.
2	7' 8"	"Ambassador" East Indian Rosewood	140,269.
2	7' 8"	"Ambassador" Walnut	129,877.
1	9' 2"	Ebony and Polished Ebony	122,130.
1	9' 2"	Walnut and Polished Walnut	128,237.
1	9' 2"	Mahogany and Polished Mahogany	127,016.
1	9' 2"	Cherry and Polished Cherry	127,628.

*For explanation of terms and prices, please see pages 59–65.

Model	Size	Style and Finish	Price*

Blüthner (continued)

1	9' 2"	White and Polished White	128,237.
1	9' 2"	"President" Polished Ebony	136,349.
1	9' 2"	"President" Polished Mahogany	141,803.
1	9' 2"	"President" Polished Walnut	143,168.
1	9' 2"	"President" Polished Bubinga	149,983.

Bohemia

Verticals

111	43"	Ebony and Polished Ebony	5,000.
111	43"	Open-pore Mahogany/Walnut/Oak	4,780.
111	43"	Polished Mahogany/Walnut	5,180.
111	43"	Polished White	5,260.
113	45"	Ebony and Polished Ebony	5,200.
113	45"	Open-pore Mahogany/Walnut/Oak	5,000.
113	45"	Polished Mahogany/Walnut	5,380.
113	45"	Polished White	5,500.
118A	47"	Continental Ebony and Polished Ebony	6,100.
118A	47"	Continental Open-pore Walnut/Mahog./Oak	5,840.
118A	47"	Continental Polished Walnut/Mahogany	6,260.
118A	47"	Continental Open-pore Cherry	6,100.
118A	47"	Continental Polished White	6,320.
122A	48"	Demi-Chippendale Ebony and Pol. Ebony	6,460.
122A	48"	Demi-Chippendale Polished Walnut/Mahog.	6,640.
122A	48"	Demi-Chippendale Polished Pomele	6,960.
122A	48"	Chippendale Ebony and Polished Ebony	7,100.
122A	48"	Chippendale Polished Walnut/Mahogany	7,320.
122A	48"	"Romance" with Mahogany Oval	7,480.
123A	48"	Ebony and Polished Ebony	6,400.
123A	48"	Open-pore Walnut/Mahogany/Oak	6,120.
123A	48"	Polished Walnut/Mahogany	6,560.
123A	48"	Open-pore Cherry	6,380.
123A	48"	Polished Pomele	6,760.
123A	48"	Polished White	6,680.
123A	48"	"Exclusive" with Mahogany Oval	6,760.
125A	49"	Ebony and Polished Ebony	6,960.
125A	49"	Polished Walnut/Mahogany	7,160.
125A	49"	Open-pore Cherry	6,960.
125A	49"	Polishsed Pomele	7,480.

Model	Size	Style and Finish	Price*
125A	49"	Polished White	7,240.
125A-BR	49"	Ebony and Polished Ebony	8,100.
125A-BR	49"	Polished Walnut/Mahogany	8,360.
125A-BR	49"	Open-pore Cherry	8,100.
125A-BR	49"	Polished Pomele	8,680.
125A-BR	49"	Polished White	8,380.
132	52"	Ebony and Polished Ebony	7,900.
132	52"	Polished Mahogany	8,700.
132BR	52"	Ebony and Polished Ebony	9,180.
132BR	52"	Polished Mahogany	10,160.

Grands

Model	Size	Style and Finish	Price*
150-B	4' 11"	Ebony and Polished Ebony	19,800.
150-B	4' 11"	Walnut and Polished Walnut	21,800.
150-B	4' 11"	Mahogany and Polished Mahogany	21,800.
150-B	4' 11"	Polished White	21,800.
156A-B	5' 2"	Ebony and Polished Ebony	20,400.
156A-B	5' 2"	Walnut and Polished Walnut	22,400.
156A-B	5' 2"	Mahogany and Polished Mahogany	22,400.
156A-B	5' 2"	Polished Pomele	26,400.
156A-B	5' 2"	Polished White	22,400.
156A-B	5' 2"	Demi-Chip. Mahogany and Pol. Mahogany	24,940.
156A-B	5' 2"	Demi-Chip. Walnut and Polished Walnut	24,940.
156A-B	5' 2"	Chippendale Mahog. and Pol. Mahogany	25,720.
156A-B	5' 2"	Chippendale Walnut and Polished Walnut	25,720.
156A-BR	5' 2"	Ebony and Polished Ebony	22,500.
156A-BR	5' 2"	Walnut and Polished Walnut	24,500.
156A-BR	5' 2"	Mahogany and Polished Mahogany	24,500.
156A-BR	5' 2"	Polished Pomele	28,540.
156A-BR	5' 2"	Polished White	24,500.
156A-BR	5' 2"	Demi-Chip. Mahogany and Pol. Mahogany	27,040.
156A-BR	5' 2"	Demi-Chip. Walnut and Polished Walnut	27,040.
156A-BR	5' 2"	Chippendale Walnut and Polished Walnut	27,800.
156A-BR	5' 2"	Chippendale Mahog. And Pol. Mahogany	27,800.
170-B	5' 7"	Ebony and Polished Ebony	22,200.
170-B	5' 7"	Walnut and Polished Walnut	24,400.
170-B	5' 7"	Mahogany and Polished Mahogany	24,400.
170-B	5' 7"	Polished White	24,400.
185A-B	6' 1"	Ebony and Polished Ebony	27,200.
185A-B	6' 1"	Walnut and Polished Walnut	27,340.
185A-B	6' 1"	Mahogany and Polished Mahogany	27,340.

*For explanation of terms and prices, please see pages 59–65.

Bohemia (continued)

Model	Size	Style and Finish	Price*
185A-B	6' 1"	*Polished Vavone*	35,780.
185A-B	6' 1"	*Polished Pyramid Mahogany*	35,780.
185A-B	6' 1"	Polished White	27,340.
185AE-B	6' 1"	Empire Polished Ebony	26,340.
185AE-B	6' 1"	Empire Walnut and Polished Walnut	28,980.
185AE-B	6' 1"	Empire Mahogany and Pol. Mahogany	28,980.
185A-BR	6' 1"	Ebony and Polished Ebony	26,940.
185A-BR	6' 1"	Walnut and Polished Walnut	29,440.
185A-BR	6' 1"	Mahogany and Polished Mahogany	29,440.
185A-BR	6' 1"	Polished White	29,440.
185A-BR	6' 1"	*Polished Vavone*	37,060.
185A-BR	6' 1"	*Polished Pyramid Mahogany*	37,060.
185AE-BR	6' 1"	Empire Ebony and Polished Ebony	28,440.
185AE-BR	6' 1"	Empire Walnut and Polished Walnut	31,080.
185AE-BR	6' 1"	Empire Mahogany and Pol. Mahogany	31,080.
225R	7' 4"	Ebony and Polished Ebony	39,740.
272R	8' 11"	Ebony and Polished Ebony	50,200.

Bösendorfer

Verticals

Model	Size	Style and Finish	Price*
130CL	*52"*	*Polished Ebony*	41,212.

Grands

Model	Size	Style and Finish	Price*
170	5' 8"	Polished Ebony	84,778.
170	5' 8"	Polished, Satin, Open-pore: Walnut, Mahogany, Pomele, Cherry, Bubinga, Wenge, White	93,500.
170	5' 8"	Polished, Satin, Open-pore: Pyramid Mahogany, Amboyna, Rio Rosewood, Burl Walnut, Birdseye Maple, Yew, Macassar	99,000.
170	5' 8"	"Johann Strauss" Polished Ebony	90,100.
170	5' 8"	"Johann Strauss," other finish	104,940.
170	5' 8"	"Franz Schubert" Polished Ebony	90,100.
170	5' 8"	"Franz Schubert," other finish	104,940.
170	5' 8"	"Senator," any finish	98,580.
170	5' 8"	"Chopin," any finish	124,020.
170	5' 8"	"Classic" any finish	104,940.
170	5' 8"	"Yacht," any finish	104,940.
185	6' 1"	Polished Ebony	86,944.

Model	Size	Style and Finish	Price*
185	6' 1"	Polished, Satin, Open-pore: Walnut, Mahogany, Pomele, Cherry, Bubinga, Wenge, White	97,848.
185	6' 1"	Polished, Satin, Open-pore: Pyramid Mahogany, Amboyna, Rio Rosewood, Burl Walnut, Birdseye Maple, Yew, Macassar	103,680.
185	6' 1"	"Johann Strauss" Polished Ebony	96,036.
185	6' 1"	"Johann Strauss" other finish	109,824.
185	6' 1"	"Franz Schubert" Polished Ebony	96,036.
185	6' 1"	"Franz Schubert" other finish	109,824.
185	6' 1"	"Senator," any finish	104,940.
185	6' 1"	"Chopin," any finish	126,988.
185	6' 1"	"Classic" any finish	109,824.
185	6' 1"	"Yacht," any finish	109,824.
185	6' 1"	"Porsche Design," Polished Ebony	119,800.
185	6' 1"	"Porsche Design," any color	131,780.
200CS	6' 7"	"Conservatory" Ebony	71,720.
200	6' 7"	Polished Ebony	95,888.
200	6' 7"	Polished, Satin, Open-pore: Walnut, Mahogany, Pomele, Cherry, Bubinga, Wenge, White	104,624.
200	6' 7"	Polished, Satin, Open-pore: Pyramid Mahogany, Amboyna, Rio Rosewood, Burl Walnut, Birdseye Maple, Yew, Macassar	109,408.
200	6' 7"	"Johann Strauss" Polished Ebony	104,624.
200	6' 7"	"Johann Strauss" other finish	122,748.
200	6' 7"	"Franz Schubert" Polished Ebony	104,624.
200	6' 7"	"Franz Schubert" other finish	122,748.
200	6' 7"	"Vienna," any finish	137,770.
200	6' 7"	"Senator," any finish	114,692.
200	6' 7"	"Chopin," any finish	137,800.
200	6' 7"	"Classic" any finish	122,748.
200	6' 7"	"Yacht," any finish	122,748.
214CS	7'	"Conservatory" Ebony	78,980.
214	7'	Polished Ebony	111,696.
214	7'	Polished, Satin, Open-pore: Walnut, Mahogany, Pomele, Cherry, Bubinga, Wenge, White	123,120.
214	7'	Polished, Satin, Open-pore: Pyramid Mahogany, Amboyna, Rio Rosewood, Burl Walnut, Birdseye Maple, Yew, Macassar	127,440.
214	7'	"Johann Strauss" Polished Ebony	120,840.

*For explanation of terms and prices, please see pages 59–65.

Bösendorfer (continued)

Model	Size	Style and Finish	Price*
214	7'	"Johann Strauss" other finish	135,200.
214	7'	"Franz Schubert" Polished Ebony	120,840.
214	7'	"Franz Schubert" other finish	135,200.
214	7'	"Vienna," any finish	154,100.
214	7'	"Senator," any finish	124,630.
214	7'	"Chopin," any finish	152,428.
214	7'	"Classic" any finish	135,200.
214	7'	"Yacht," any finish	135,200.
214	7'	"Porsche Design," Polished Ebony	143,800.
214	7'	"Porsche Design," any color	158,180.
225	7' 4"	Polished Ebony	117,104.
225	7' 4"	Polished, Satin, Open-pore: Walnut, Mahogany, Pomele, Cherry, Bubinga, Wenge, White	127,504.
225	7' 4"	Polished, Satin, Open-pore: Pyramid Mahogany, Amboyna, Rio Rosewood, Burl Walnut, Birdseye Maple, Yew, Macassar	132,912.
225	7' 4"	"Johann Strauss" Polished Ebony	127,504.
225	7' 4"	"Johann Strauss" other finish	149,036.
225	7' 4"	"Franz Schubert" Polished Ebony	127,504.
225	7' 4"	"Franz Schubert" other finish	149,036.
225	7' 4"	"Vienna," any finish	165,600.
225	7' 4"	"Senator," any finish	131,000.
225	7' 4"	"Chopin," any finish	158,788.
225	7' 4"	"Classic" any finish	149,036.
225	7' 4"	"Yacht," any finish	149,036.
170-225		Chippendale, any finish, add'l	4,240.
170-225		Louis XV, any finish, add'l	21,200.
170-225		Baroque, any finish, add'l	21,200.
280	9' 2"	Polished Ebony	151,840.
280	9' 2"	Polished, Satin, Open-pore: Walnut, Mahogany, Pomele, Cherry, Bubinga, Wenge, White	169,128.
280	9' 2"	Polished, Satin, Open-pore: Pyramid Mahogany, Amboyna, Rio Rosewood, Burl Walnut, Birdseye Maple, Yew, Macassar	175,608.
280	9' 2"	"Johann Strauss" Polished Ebony	165,996.
280	9' 2"	"Johann Strauss" other finish	188,680.
280	9' 2"	"Franz Schubert" Polished Ebony	165,996.
280	9' 2"	"Franz Schubert" other finish	188,680.

Model	Size	Style and Finish	Price*
280	9' 2"	"Vienna," any finish	209,300.
280	9' 2"	"Senator," any finish	170,568.
280	9' 2"	"Chopin," any finish	203,096.
280	9' 2"	"Classic" any finish	188,680.
280	9' 2"	"Yacht," any finish	188,680.
280	9' 2"	"Porsche Design," Polished Ebony	191,000.
280	9' 2"	"Porsche Design," any color	210,100.
290	9' 6"	Polished Ebony	172,640.
290	9' 6"	Polished, Satin, Open-pore: Walnut, Mahogany, Pomele, Cherry, Bubinga, Wenge, White	191,160.
290	9' 6"	Polished, Satin, Open-pore: Pyramid Mahogany, Amboyna, Rio Rosewood, Burl Walnut, Birdseye Maple, Yew, Macassar	198,072.
290	9' 6"	"Johann Strauss" Polished Ebony	187,620.
290	9' 6"	"Johann Strauss" other finish	209,880.
290	9' 6"	"Franz Schubert" Polished Ebony	187,620.
290	9' 6"	"Franz Schubert" other finish	209,880.
290	9' 6"	"Vienna," any finish	232,300.
290	9' 6"	"Senator," any finish	191,992.
290	9' 6"	"Chopin," any finish	228,960.
290	9' 6"	"Classic" any finish	209,880.
290	9' 6"	"Yacht," any finish	209,880.
280-290		Chippendale, any finish, add'l	5,300.
280-290		Louis XV, any finish, add'l	25,440.
280-290		Baroque, any finish, add'l	25,440.

Boston

Verticals

Model	Size	Style and Finish	Price*
UP-118E	46"	Ebony and Polished Ebony	9,820.
UP-118E	46"	Walnut	10,990.
UP-118E	46"	Polished Walnut/Mahogany	11,220.
UP-118E	46"	Polished White	11,060.
UP-118A	46"	Art Deco Aniegre	7,990.
UP-118S	46"	Open-Pore Honey Oak/Black Oak/Red Oak	6,140.
UP-118S	46"	Mahogany	7,600.
UP-126E	50"	Ebony and Polished Ebony	11,920.
UP-126E	50"	Polished Mahogany	13,760.
UP-132E	52"	Polished Ebony	13,100.

*For explanation of terms and prices, please see pages 59–65.

Boston (continued)
Grands

Model	Size	Style and Finish	Price*
GP-156	5' 1"	Ebony and Polished Ebony	17,190.
GP-163	5' 4"	Ebony	20,540.
GP-163	5' 4"	Polished Ebony	21,100.
GP-163	5' 4"	Mahogany	22,480.
GP-163	5' 4"	Polished Mahogany	23,100.
GP-163	5' 4"	Walnut	22,680.
GP-163	5' 4"	Polished Walnut	23,360.
GP-163	5' 4"	Polished White/Ivory	21,680.
GP-178	5' 10"	Ebony	23,700.
GP-178	5' 10"	Polished Ebony	24,300.
GP-178	5' 10"	Mahogany	25,340.
GP-178	5' 10"	Polished Mahogany	26,040.
GP-178	5' 10"	Walnut	25,640.
GP-178	5' 10"	Polished Walnut	26,520.
GP-178	5' 10"	Polished White/Ivory	24,820.
GP-193	6' 4"	Ebony	30,120.
GP-193	6' 4"	Polished Ebony	30,900.
GP-193	6' 4"	Walnut	33,560.
GP-193	6' 4"	Polished Mahogany	33,800.
GP-193	6' 4"	Polished White	32,520.
GP-215	7' 1"	Ebony	38,960.
GP-215	7' 1"	Polished Ebony	39,900.

Breitmann

Verticals

Model	Size	Style and Finish	Price*
P110	44"	Polished Ebony	3,060.
P110	44"	Polished Mahogany/Brown Mahogany	3,120.
P120	48"	Polished Ebony	3,502.
P120	48"	Polished Mahogany/Brown Mahogany	3,640.
P122	49"	Polished Ebony	3,924.
P122	49"	Polished Mahogany/Brown Mahogany	4,126.
P130	52"	Polished Ebony	4,220.
P130	52"	Polished Mahogany/Brown Mahogany	4,560.
P130	52"	Polished White	4,320.

Grands

Model	Size	Style and Finish	Price*
B16	5' 2"	Polished Ebony	9,450.
B16	5' 2"	Polished White	9,600.

Cable, Hobart M.

Model numbers ending in "D" indicate slow-close fallboard.

Verticals

Model	Size	Style and Finish	Price*
UH 09	43"	Continental Polished Ebony	2,870.
UH 09	43"	Continental Cherry/Mahogany	2,930.
UH 09	43"	Continental Polished Mahogany/Walnut	2,990.
UH 09	43"	Continental Polished Ivory/White	2,990.
UH 09A	43"	Continental Polished Ebony	2,680.
UH 09A	43"	Continental Polished Mahogany	2,800.
UH 09L	43"	Continental (w/toe) Polished Ebony	2,950.
UH 09L	43"	Continental (w/toe) Pol, Mahogany/Walnut	3,070.
UH 09L	43"	Continental (w/toe) Polished White	3,070.
CH 12F	44"	French Provincial Cherry/Brown Oak	3,370.
CH 12F1	44"	French Provincial Cherry/Brown Oak	3,190.
CH 12FD	44"	French Provincial Cherry/Brown Oak	3,490.
CH 12M	44"	Mediterranean Cherry/Brown Oak	3,370.
CH 12M1	44"	Mediterranean Cherry/Brown Oak	3,190.
CH 12MD	44"	Mediterranean Cherry/Brown Oak	3,490.
UH 12F	44"	Cherry/Mahogany	3,260.
UH 12T	44"	Polished Ebony	3,080.
UH 12T	44"	Mahogany/Walnut/Cherry	3,140.
UH 12T	44"	Polished Mahogany/Walnut	3,200.
UH 12T	44"	Polished Ivory and White	3,200.
CH 13F1D	44-1/2"	French Designer Cherry/Dark Cherry	3,790.
CH 13F1D	44-1/2"	French Designer Brown Oak	3,790.
CH 13MD	44-1/2"	Designer Cherry/Mahogany	3,590.
CH 13M1D	44-1/2"	Designer Cherry/Dark Cherry	3,790.
CH 13M1D	44-1/2"	Designer Brown Oak	3,790.
CH 16ATD	45-1/2"	Cherry	3,990.
CH 16FPD	45-1/2"	French Provincial Cherry/Brown Oak	3,790.
CH 16IPD	45-1/2"	Italian Provincial Cherry	3,790.
CH 16QAD	45-1/2"	Queen Anne Cherry	4,090.
UH 16I	45-1/2"	Polished Walnut	3,160.
UH 16ST	45-1/2"	Brown Oak/Cherry	3,200.
UH 16STL	45-1/2"	Brown Oak/Cherry	3,500.
CH 19F	47"	Country French Cherry/Brown Oak	3,700.
CH 19FD	47"	Country French Cherry/Brown Oak	3,820.
CH 19M	47"	Mediterranean Brown Oak/Cherry	3,700.
CH 19MD	47"	Cherry/Brown Oak	3,820.
CH 19M1D	47"	Cherry	3,820.

*For explanation of terms and prices, please see pages 59—65.

Model	Size	Style and Finish	Price*

Cable, Hobart M. (continued)

CH 19QAD	47"	Queen Anne Cherry	4,190.
UH 19F	47"	Demi-Chippendale Polished Ebony	3,320.
UH 19F	47"	Demi-Chippendale Other Finishes (Satin)	3,380.
UH 19F	47"	Demi-Chippendale Other Finished (Pol.)	3,440.
UH 19FC	47"	Chippendale Polished Mahogany/Walnut	3,500.
UH 19ST	47"	Polished Ebony	3,200.
UH 19ST	47"	Oak/Brown Oak/Cherry	3,260.
UH 19ST	47"	Polished Mahogany/Walnut	3,320.
UH 19ST	47"	Polished White	3,320.
UH 19T	47"	Polished Ebony	3,200.
UH 19T	47"	Cherry/Brown Oak	3,260.
UH 19T	47"	Polished Mahogany/Walnut	3,320.
UH 19T	47"	Polished Ivory	3,320.
UH 20T	47"	Designer Polished Ebony	3,490.
UH 22F	48"	Demi-Chippendale Polished Ebony	3,490.
UH 22F	48"	Demi-Chippendale Polished Mahogany	3,610.
UH 22F	48"	Polished Walnut	3,610.
UH 22FD	48"	Polished Mahogany/Walnut	3,730.
UH 22FD	48"	Polished Ivory/White	3,730.
UH 22T	48"	Polished Ebony	3,370.
UH 22T	48"	Polished Mahogany/Walnut	3,490.
UH 22T	48"	Polished White	3,490.
UH 22TD	48"	Polished Ebony	3,490.
UH 22TD	48"	Polished Mahogany/Walnut	3,610.
UH 22TD	48"	Polished Ivory/White	3,610.
UH 23FD	48-1/2"	Designer Polished Walnut	3,860.
UH 23TD	48-1/2"	Designer Polished Ebony	3,620.
UH 23TD	48-1/2"	Designer Polished Mahogany/Walnut	3,740.
UH 32F	52"	French Provincial Polished Ebony	3,740.
UH 32F	52"	French Provincial Pol. Mahogany/Walnut	3,860.
UH 32FD	52"	Chippendale Polished Ebony	3,860.
UH 32FD	52"	Chippendale Polished Mahogany/Walnut	3,980.
UH 32T	52"	Polished Ebony	3,620.
UH 32T	52"	Polished Mahogany/Walnut	3,740.
UH 32TD	52"	Polished Mahogany/Walnut	3,860.

Grands

GH 42	4' 8"	Polished Ebony	8,420.
GH 42	4' 8"	Polished White	8,620.
GH 42	4' 8"	Mahogany/Walnut/Oak	9,020.

Model	Size	Style and Finish	Price*
GH 42	4' 8"	Polished Mahogany/Walnut/Brown Oak	8,820.
GH 42D	4' 8"	Ebony	8,740.
GH 42D	4' 8"	Polished Ebony	8,540.
GH 42D	4' 8"	Cherry/Mahogany	9,140.
GH 42D	4' 8"	Polished Mahogany/Walnut/Cherry	8,940.
GH 42D	4' 8"	Polished Bubinga	9,540.
GH 42D	4' 8"	Polished Ivory	8,740.
GH 42F	4' 8"	French Provincial Polished Ebony	9,020.
GH 42F	4' 8"	French Provincial Cherry/Walnut	9,620.
GH 42F	4' 8"	French Provincial Pol. Mahogany/Walnut	9,420.
GH 42FD	4' 8"	French Provincial Cherry/Walnut	9,740.
GH 42FD	4' 8"	French Provincial Polished Cherry/Walnut	9,540.
GH 52	5'	Ebony	9,460.
GH 52	5'	Polished Ebony	9,260.
GH 52	5'	Polished Ivory/White	9,460.
GH 52	5'	Mahogany	9,860.
GH 52	5'	Polished Mahogany/Walnut	9,660.
GH 52D	5'	Ebony	9,580.
GH 52D	5'	Polished Ebony	9,380.
GH 52D	5'	Mahogany/Cherry	9,980.
GH 52D	5'	Polished Mahogany/Walnut/Cherry	9,780.
GH 52F	5'	French Provincial Mahogany/Walnut	10,380.
GH 52FD	5'	French Provincial Mahogany	10,580.
GH 52FD	5'	French Provincial Pol. Mahogany/Walnut	10,380.
GH 62	5' 4"	Ebony	10,490.
GH 62	5' 4"	Polished Ebony	10,290.
GH 62	5' 4"	Polished Ivory	10,490.
GH 62	5' 4"	Polished Mahogany/Walnut/Brown Oak	10,690.
GH 62	5' 4"	Polished White	10,690.
GH 62D	5' 4"	Ebony	10,610.
GH 62D	5' 4"	Polished Ebony	10,410.
GH 62D	5' 4"	Cherry/Walnut	11,010.
GH 62D	5' 4"	Polished Mahogany/Walnut	10,810.
GH 62D	5' 4"	Polished Bubinga	11,410.
GH 62F	5' 4"	French Provincial Ebony	11,090.
GH 62F	5' 4"	French Provincial Polished White	11,090.
GH 62F	5' 4"	French Provincial Cherry/Mahogany	11,490.
GH 62F	5' 4"	French Provincial Pol. Mahogany/Walnut	11,290.
GH 62FD	5' 4"	French Provincial Cherry	11,610.
GH 62FD	5' 4"	French Provincial Polished Mahogany	11,410.
GH 62L	5' 4"	Louis XVI Polished Ebony	10,770.

*For explanation of terms and prices, please see pages 59–65.

Model	Size	Style and Finish	Price*

Cable, Hobart M. (continued)

Model	Size	Style and Finish	Price*
GH 72	5' 8"	Ebony	11,520.
GH 72	5' 8"	Polished Ebony	11,320.
GH 72	5' 8"	Polished Ivory	11,520.
GH 72	5' 8"	Walnut	11,920.
GH 72	5' 8"	Polished Mahogany/Walnut/Brown Oak	11,720.
GH 72	5' 8"	Polished White	11,720.
GH 72D	5' 8"	Ebony	11,640.
GH 72D	5' 8"	Polished Ebony	11,440.
GH 72D	5' 8"	Mahogany	12,040.
GH 72D	5' 8"	Polished Mahogany/Walnut	11,840.
GH 72D	5' 8"	Polished Bubinga	12,440.
GH 72FD	5' 8"	French Provincial Polished Mahogany	12,440.
GH 72LD	5' 8"	Louis XVI Polished Ebony	11,920.
GH 72LD	5' 8"	Louis XVI Polished Mahogany	12,320.
GH 87	6' 2"	Ebony	12,540.
GH 87	6' 2"	Polished Ebony	12,340.
GH 87	6' 2"	Polished Mahogany/Walnut	12,740.
GH 87D	6' 2"	Ebony	12,660.
GH 87D	6' 2"	Polished Ebony	12,460.
GH 87D	6' 2"	Mahogany	13,060.
GH 87D	6' 2"	Polished Mahogany/Walnut	12,860.
GH 87F	6' 2"	French Provincial Cherry	13,540.
GH 87F	6' 2"	French Provincial Pol. Mahogany/Walnut	13,340.
GH 87FD	6' 2"	French Provincial Cherry	13,660.
GH 87FD	6' 2"	French Provincial Polished Mahogany	13,460.
GH 87L	6' 2"	Louis XVI Polished Ebony	12,820.
GH 87LD	6' 2"	Louis XVI Ebony	13,140.
GH 87LD	6' 2"	Louis XVI Polished Ebony	12,940.
GH 87LD	6' 2"	Louis XVI Mahogany	13,540.
GH 87LD	6' 2"	Louis XVI Polished Mahogany	13,340.

Charles R. Walter — see "Walter, Charles R."

Chase, A. B.

Verticals

Model	Size	Style and Finish	Price*
EV-112	44"	Continental Polished Ebony	2,580.
EV-112	44"	Continental Polished Mahogany	2,700.

Model	Size	Style and Finish	Price*
EV-113	45"	Polished Ebony	2,780.
EV-113	45"	Polished Mahogany	2,900.
EV-115CB	45"	Chippendale Polished Mahogany	3,100.
EV-121	48"	Polished Ebony	3,180.
EV-121	48"	Polished Mahogany	3,300.

Grands

Model	Size	Style and Finish	Price*
EV-152	5'	Polished Ebony	7,780.
EV-152	5'	Polished Mahogany/Walnut	8,280.
EV-152	5'	Polished Sapele	8,480.
EV-152	5'	Polished White	8,280.
EV-165	5' 5"	Polished Ebony	8,780.
EV-165	5' 5"	Polished Mahogany/Walnut	9,280.
EV-185	6' 1"	Polished Ebony	10,780.
EV-185	6' 1"	Polished Mahogany	11,280.

Conover Cable

Verticals

Model	Size	Style and Finish	Price*
CC-142	42"	Continental Polished Ebony	2,750.
CC-142	42"	Continental Walnut/Cherry	2,850.
CC-142	42"	Continental Polished Mahogany/Walnut	2,850.
CC-142	42"	Continental Polished Ivory	2,850.
CC-043F	43"	French Provincial Cherry	2,990.
CC-043T	43"	Mahogany	2,990.
CC-145	45"	Ebony	3,190.
CC-145	45"	Polished Ebony	3,190.
CC-145	45"	Mahogany/Walnut/Cherry	3,190.
CC-145	45"	Polished Mahogany	3,190.
CC-247	46-1/2"	Polished Ebony	4,700.
CC-247	46-1/2"	Walnut	4,700.
CC-121F	48"	French Provincial Polished Ebony	4,190.
CC-121F	48"	French Provincial Polished Mahogany	4,390.
CC-121M	48"	Mediterranean Polished Ebony	3,990.
CC-121M	48"	Mediterranean Polished Mahogany	4,270.

Grands

Model	Size	Style and Finish	Price*
CCIG-50	4' 11-1/2"	Ebony	8,590.
CCIG-50	4' 11-1/2"	Polished Ebony	8,390.
CCIG-50	4' 11-1/2"	Polished Mahogany	8,990.
CCIG-50KBF	4' 11-1/2"	French Provincial Polished Cherry	10,390.
CCIG-54	5' 3"	Ebony	9,790.

*For explanation of terms and prices, please see pages 59–65.

Conover Cable (continued)

CCIG-54	5' 3"	Polished Ebony	9,590.
CCIG-54	5' 3"	Polished Mahogany	10,190.
CCIG-57	5' 7"	Ebony	10,590.
CCIG-57	5' 7"	Polished Ebony	10,390.
CCIG-57	5' 7"	Polished Mahogany	10,990.
CCIG-61	6' 1"	Ebony	11,390.
CCIG-61	6' 1"	Polished Ebony	11,190.
CCIG-61	6' 1"	Polished Mahogany	11,790.

Ebel, Carl

Verticals

LF-109AB	43"	Continental Polished Ebony	4,180.
LF-109AC	43"	Continental Polished Mahogany/Walnut	4,270.
LF-109AC	43"	Continental Polished White	4,270.
LF-109AF	43"	Continental Polished Ebony w/Molding	4,480.
LF-109AS	43"	Continental Cherry/Oak	4,270.
LF-109BB	43"	Polished Ebony (straight leg)	4,480.
LF-109BC	43"	Polished Mahogany/Walnut (straight leg)	4,480.
LF-109BC	43"	Polished White (straight leg)	4,480.
LF-109BF	43"	Pol. Mahogany w/Molding (straight leg)	4,630.
LF-109BF	43"	Pol. Walnut w/Molding (straight leg)	4,630.
LF-109BF	43"	Oak w/Molding (straight leg)	4,630.
LF-109EF	43"	Polished Ebony (curved leg)	4,630.
LF-109EF	43"	Polished Mahogany/Walnut (curved leg)	4,780.
LF-113G	44"	Queen Anne or Mediterranean Walnut	5,340.
LF-113G	44"	Queen Anne or Mediterranean Cherry/Oak	5,340.
LM-116EF	46"	Chippendale Polished Ebony	4,780.
LM-116EF	46"	Chippendale Pol. Mahogany w/Molding	4,990.
LM-116EF	46"	Chippendale Pol. Walnut w/Molding	4,990.
LM-116H	46"	Polished Ebony (straight leg)	4,780.
LM-116H	46"	Polished Mahogany/Walnut (straight leg)	5,090.
LM-116H	46"	Polished Oak (straight leg)	5,090.
LM-116H	46"	Polished White (straight leg)	5,090.
LM-116H	46"	Pol. Ebony w/Mahog. Or Walnut Accents	4,780.
LM-117CW	46"	Walnut	5,980.
LM-117GW	46"	Walnut (curved leg)	5,980.
LT-122BB	48"	Polished Ebony (straight leg)	5,530.
LT-122BC	48"	Polished Mahogany/Walnut (straight leg)	5,830.

Model	Size	Style and Finish	Price*
LT-122BC	48"	Polished White (straight leg)	5,830.
LT-122BF	48"	Polished Ebony w/Molding (straight leg)	5,980.
LT-122BF	48"	Pol. Mahogany w/Molding (straight leg)	5,980.
LT-122BF	48"	Polished Walnut w/Molding (straight leg)	5,980.

Grands

Model	Size	Style and Finish	Price*
F-150BB	4' 11"	Polished Ebony	9,990.
F-150BC	4' 11"	Polished Mahogany/Walnut	10,490.
F-150BC	4' 11"	Polished White	10,490.

Essex

Verticals

Model	Size	Style and Finish	Price*
EUP-107C	42"	Continental Polished Ebony	5,190.
EUP-111E	44"	European Polished Ebony	5,750.
EUP-111E	44"	European Polished Mahogany	5,890.
EUP-111E	44"	European Polished Walnut	5,950.
EUP-111E	44"	European Polished White	5,790.
EUP-111F	44"	French Provincial Cherry	6,270.
EUP-111M	44"	Modern Walnut	5,990.
EUP-111R	44"	English Regency Mahogany	5,830.
EUP-111T	44"	Ash	5,870.

Grands

Model	Size	Style and Finish	Price*
EGP-161	5' 3"	Ebony	14,060.
EGP-161	5' 3"	Polished Ebony	13,790.
EGP-161	5' 3"	Mahogany	15,180.
EGP-161	5' 3"	Polished Mahogany	14,900.
EGP-161	5' 3"	Walnut	15,580.
EGP-161	5' 3"	Cherry	15,820.
EGP-161	5' 3"	Oak	15,500.
EGP-161	5' 3"	Polished White	13,960.
EGP-161N	5' 3"	Neo-Classic Mahogany	17,700.
EGP-161N	5' 3"	Neo-Classic Polished Mahogany	17,500.
EGP-161N	5' 3"	Neo-Classic Cherry	18,500.
EGP-183	6'	Ebony	18,100.
EGP-183	6'	Polished Ebony	17,840.
EGP-183	6'	Polished Mahogany	19,050.
EGP-183	6'	Walnut	19,850.

*For explanation of terms and prices, please see pages 59–65.

Estonia

Prices include Jansen adjustable artist bench.

Grands

Model	Size	Style and Finish	Price
168	5' 6"	Ebony and Polished Ebony	27,000.
168	5' 6"	Mahogany and Polished Mahogany	29,300.
168	5' 6"	Walnut and Polished Walnut	29,300.
168	5' 6"	Bubinga and Polished Bubinga	31,850.
168	5' 6"	"Hidden Beauty" Pol. Ebony w/Bubinga	30,000.
190	6' 3"	Ebony and Polished Ebony	33,000.
190	6' 3"	Mahogany and Polished Mahogany	35,560.
190	6' 3"	Walnut and Polished Walnut	35,560.
190	6' 3"	Bubinga and Polished Bubinga	38,400.
190	6' 3"	"Hidden Beauty" Pol. Ebony w/Bubinga	35,150.
273	9'	Ebony and Polished Ebony	80,000.

Everett

Verticals

Model	Size	Style and Finish	Price
EV-112	44"	Continental Polished Ebony	2,580.
EV-112	44"	Continental Polished Mahogany	2,700.
EV-113	45"	Polished Ebony	2,780.
EV-113	45"	Polished Mahogany	2,900.
EV-115CB	45"	Chippendale Polished Mahogany	3,100.
EV-121	48"	Polished Ebony	3,180.
EV-121	48"	Polished Mahogany	3,300.

Grands

Model	Size	Style and Finish	Price
EV-152	5'	Polished Ebony	7,780.
EV-152	5'	Polished Mahogany/Walnut	8,280.
EV-152	5'	Polished Sapele	8,480.
EV-152	5'	Polished White	8,280.
EV-165	5' 5"	Polished Ebony	8,780.
EV-165	5' 5"	Polished Mahogany/Walnut	9,280.
EV-185	6' 1"	Polished Ebony	10,780.
EV-185	6' 1"	Polished Mahogany	11,280.

Falcone

Model numbers ending in "D" indicate slow-close fallboard.

Verticals

Model	Size	Style and Finish	Price*
UF 09	43"	Continental Polished Ebony	2,870.
UF 09	43"	Continental Cherry/Sapele	2,930.
UF 09	43"	Continental Polished Mahogany/Walnut	2,990.
UF 09	43"	Continental Polished Ivory	2,990.
UF 09L	43"	Polished Ebony	2,950.
UF 09L	43"	Polished Mahogany/Walnut	3,070.
CF 12FD	44"	French Provincial Brown Oak/Cherry	3,490.
CF 12MD	44"	Mediterranean Brown Oak/Cherry	3,490.
UF 12F	44"	French Provincial Polished Ebony	3,200.
UF 12F	44"	French Provincial Cherry/Sapele	3.260.
UF 12F	44"	French Provincial Pol. Mahogany/Walnut	3,320.
UF 12F	44"	French Provincial Polished Ivory	3,320.
UF 12T	44"	Polished Ebony	3,080.
UF 12T	44"	Cherry/Walnut/Sapele	3,140.
UF 12T	44"	Polished Mahogany/Walnut	3,200.
UF 12T	44"	Polished Ivory/White	3,200.
CF 13FD	44-1/2"	French Designer Cherry/Mahogany	3,590.
CF 13F1D	44-1/2"	French Provincial Cherry/Mahogany	3,790.
CF 13MD	44-1/2"	Cherry/Mahogany	3,590.
CF 13M1D	44-1/2"	Cherry/Mahogany	3,790.
CF 16ATD	45-1/2"	Cherry	3,990.
CF 16FD	45-1/2"	French Provincial Cherry/Brown Oak	3,770.
CF 16FPD	45-1/2"	French Provincial Cherry/Brown Oak	3,790.
CF 16IPD	45-1/2"	Italian Provincial Cherry/Walnut	3,790.
CF 16QAD	45-1/2"	Queen Anne Cherry/Brown Oak	4,090.
CF 19FD	47"	Country French Cherry	3,820.
CF 19F1D	47"	French Provincial Cherry/Brown Oak	3,820.
CF 19MD	47"	Mediterranean Cherry/Brown Oak	3,820.
CF 19M1D	47"	Mediterranean Cherry/Brown Oak	3,820.
CF 19QAD	47"	Queen Anne Cherry/Brown Oak	4,190.
UF 19F	47"	Demi-Chippendale Polished Ebony	3,320.
UF 19F	47"	Demi-Chippendale Cherry/Sapele	3,380.
UF 19F	47"	Demi-Chippendale Pol. Mahogany/Walnut	3,440.
UF 19F	47"	Demi-Chippendale Pol. Cherry	3,440.
UF 19F	47"	Demi-Chippendale Polished Ivory/White	3,440.
UF 19T	47"	Polished Ebony	3,200.
UF 19T	47"	Polished Mahogany	3,320.

*For explanation of terms and prices, please see pages 59–65.

Model	Size	Style and Finish	Price*

Falcone (continued)

Model	Size	Style and Finish	Price*
UF 19T	47"	Polished Ivory/White	3,320.
UF 20T	47	Designer Polished Ebony	3,490.
UF 20T	47"	Designer Polished Mahogany/Walnut	3,610.
UF 20T	47"	Designer Polished Ivory	3,610.
UF 23FD	48"	French Provincial Polished Ebony	3,740.
UF 23FD	48"	French Provincial Cherry/Sapele	3,800.
UF 23FD	48"	French Provincial Pol. Mahogany/Walnut	3,860.
UF 23TD	48"	Designer Polished Ebony	3,620.
UF 23TD	48"	Designer Polished Mahogany/Walnut	3,740.
UF 23TD	48"	Designer Polished Ivory	3,740.
UF 26T	48"	Ebony	3,900.
UF 26T	48"	Polished Ebony	3,740.
UF 32FD	52"	Chippendale Polished Ebony	3,860.
UF 32FD	52"	Chippendale Polished Mahogany	3,980.
UF 32TD	52	Polished Ebony	3,740.
UF 32TD	52"	Polished Mahogany/Walnut	3,860.

Grands

Model	Size	Style and Finish	Price*
GF 42	4' 8"	Polished Ebony	8,420.
GF 42	4' 8"	Polished Ivory/White	8,620.
GF 42	4' 8"	Polished Cherry/Mahogany/Walnut	8,820.
GF 52	5'	Polished Ebony	9,260.
GF 52	5'	Polished Ivory/White	9,460.
GF 52	5'	Polished Mahogany/Walnut	9,660.
GF 52F	5'	French Provincial Cherry	10,580.
GF 52F	5'	French Provincial Pol. Mahogany/Walnut	10,380.
GF 62	5' 4"	Polished Ebony	10,290.
GF 62	5' 4"	Polished Ivory	10,490.
GF 62	5' 4"	Polished Mahogany/Walnut	10,690.
GF 62F	5' 4"	French Provincial Polished Mahogany	11,290.
GF 62F	5' 4"	French Provincial Polished Ivory	11,210.
GF 72	5' 8"	Polished Ebony	11,320.
GF 72	5' 8"	Polished Mahogany/Walnut	11,720.
GF 72F	5' 8"	French Provincial Polished Mahogany	12,320.
GF 72L	5' 8"	Louis XVI Polished Mahogany	12,200.
GF 87	6' 2"	Polished Ebony	12,340.
GF 87	6' 2"	Polished Mahogany	12,740.
GF 87L	6' 2"	Louis XVI Polished Mahogany	13,220.

All grand models above available with slow-close fallboard for add'l 120.
Some satin finishes also available.

Model	Size	Style and Finish	Price*
GF 87FD	6' 2"	French Provincial Polished Ebony	13,060.
GF 87FD	6' 2"	French Provincial Cherry/Mahogany	13,660.
GF 87FD	6' 2"	French Provincial Pol. Cherry/Mahogany	13,460.
GF 208D	6' 10"	Ebony	15,800.
GF 208D	6' 10"	Polished Ebony	15,600.
GF 228D	7' 6"	Ebony	19,800.
GF 228D	7' 6"	Polished Ebony	19,600.
GF 278D	9' 2"	Ebony	47,800.
GF 278D	9' 2"	Polished Ebony	47,600.

Falcone Georgian Grands

Model	Size	Style and Finish	Price*
FG 42D	4' 8"	Ebony	8,980.
FG 42D	4' 8"	Polished Ebony	8,780.
FG 42D	4' 8"	Polished Ivory/White	8,980.
FG 42D	4' 8"	Cherry/Mahogany/Walnut	9,180.
FG 42D	4' 8"	Polished Cherry/Mahogany/Walnut	9,180.
FG 42D	4' 8"	Polished Bubinga	9,780.
FG 42FD	4' 8"	French Provincial Mahogany	9,980.
FG 42FD	4' 8"	French Provincial Polished Mahogany	9,780.
FG 52D	5'	Ebony	9,820.
FG 52D	5'	Polished Ebony	9,620.
FG 52D	5'	Polished White	10,020.
FG 52D	5'	Cherry/Mahogany/Walnut	10,220.
FG 52D	5'	Polished Cherry/Mahogany/Walnut	10,020.
FG 52D	5'	Polished Bubinga	10,620.
FG 52FD	5'	French Provincial Polished Ebony	10,220.
FG 52FD	5'	French Provincial Polished Ivory	10,580.
FG 52FD	5'	French Provincial Cherry/Mahogany	10,820.
FG 52FD	5'	French Provincial Pol. Cherry	10,620.
FG 52FD	5'	French Provincial Pol. Mahogany/Walnut	10,620.
FG 62D	5' 4"	Ebony	11,180.
FG 62D	5' 4"	Polished Ebony	10,980.
FG 62D	5' 4"	Polished Ivory/White	11,180.
FG 62D	5' 4"	Cherry/Mahogany/Walnut	11,580.
FG 62D	5' 4"	Polished Mahogany/Walnut	11,380.
FG 62D	5' 4"	Polished Bubinga	11,980.
FG 62FD	5' 4"	French Provincial Cherry/Mahogany	12,180.
FG 62FD	5' 4"	French Provincial Pol. Cherry/Mahogany	11,980.
FG 72D	5' 8"	Ebony	12,210.
FG 72D	5' 8"	Polished Ebony	12,010.
FG 72D	5' 8"	Polished Ivory/White	12,210.

*For explanation of terms and prices, please see pages 59–65.

Falcone (continued)

Model	Size	Style and Finish	Price*
FG 72D	5' 8"	Mahogany	12,610.
FG 72D	5' 8"	Polished Mahogany/Walnut	12,410.
FG 72D	5' 8"	Polished Bubinga	12,610.
FG 72FD	5' 8"	French Provincial Polished Ivory	12,810.
FG 72FD	5' 8"	French Provincial Pol. Mahogany/Walnut	13,010.
FG 72FD	5' 8"	French Provincial Polished Cherry	13,010.
FG 72LD	5' 8"	Louis XVI Polished Ebony	12,490.
FG 72LD	5' 8"	Louis XVI Mahogany	13,090.
FG 72LD	5' 8"	Louis XVI Polished Mahogany	12,890.
FG 87D	6' 2"	Ebony	13,230.
FG 87D	6' 2"	Polished Ebony	13,030.
FG 87D	6' 2"	Polished Mahogany/Walnut	13,430.
FG 87D	6' 2"	Polished Bubinga	13,630.
FG 87FD	6' 2"	French Provincial Polished Ebony	13,630.
FG 87FD	6' 2"	French Provincial Pol. Cherry/Mahogany	14,030.
FG 87LD	6' 2"	Louis XVI Ebony	13,710.
FG 87LD	6' 2"	Louis XVI Polished Ebony	13,510.
FG 87LD	6' 2"	Louis XVI Polished Ivory	13,710.
FG 87LD	6' 2"	Louis XVI Polished Mahogany	13,910.
FG 208D	6' 10"	Ebony	16,180.
FG 208D	6' 10"	Polished Ebony	15,980.
FG 208HLD	6' 10"	Mahogany	16,600.
FG 228D	7' 6"	Ebony	20,180.
FG 228D	7' 6"	Polished Ebony	19,980.
FG 278D	9' 2"	Ebony	47,800.
FG 278D	9' 2"	Polished Ebony	47,600.

Fazioli

Fazioli is willing to make custom-designed cases with exotic veneers, marquetry, and other embellishments. Prices on request to Fazioli.

Grands

Model	Size	Style and Finish	Price*
F156	5' 2"	Ebony and Polished Ebony	84,400.
F156	5' 2"	Walnut	88,400.
F156	5' 2"	Polished Walnut	90,600.
F156	5' 2"	Polished Pyramid Mahogany	93,400.
F156	5' 2"	Cherry	88,400.
F156	5' 2"	Polished Cherry	90,600.
F183	6'	Ebony and Polished Ebony	97,500.

Model	Size	Style and Finish	Price*
F183	6'	Walnut	102,850.
F183	6'	Polished Walnut	104,920.
F183	6'	Polished Pyramid Mahogany	108,600.
F183	6'	Cherry	102,850.
F183	6'	Polished Cherry	104,920.
F212	6' 11"	Ebony and Polished Ebony	112,360.
F212	6' 11"	Walnut	117,960.
F212	6' 11"	Polished Walnut	120,600.
F212	6' 11"	Polished Pyramid Mahogany	124,660.
F212	6' 11"	Cherry	117,960.
F212	6' 11"	Polished Cherry	120,600.
F228	7' 6"	Ebony and Polished Ebony	128,840.
F228	7' 6"	Walnut	135,200.
F228	7' 6"	Polished Walnut	137,400.
F228	7' 6"	Polished Pyramid Mahogany	143,800.
F228	7' 6"	Cherry	135,200.
F228	7' 6"	Polished Cherry	137,400.
F278	9' 2"	Ebony and Polished Ebony	167,200.
F278	9' 2"	Walnut	175,600.
F278	9' 2"	Polished Walnut	179,600.
F278	9' 2"	Polished Pyramid Mahogany	185,680.
F278	9' 2"	Cherry	175,600.
F278	9' 2"	Polished Cherry	179,600.
F308	10' 2"	Ebony and Polished Ebony	198,400.
F308	10' 2"	Walnut	206,700.
F308	10' 2"	Polished Walnut	208,200.
F308	10' 2"	Polished Pyramid Mahogany	217,400.
F308	10' 2"	Cherry	206,700.
F308	10' 2"	Polished Cherry	208,200.
All models		*Fourth Pedal, add'l*	9,150.
All models		*Third and Fourth Pedals (set), add'l*	10,760.
All models		*Magnetic Balanced Action, add'l*	12,200.

Feurich

Prices do not include bench.

Verticals

F 123	49"	Polished Ebony	26,914.
F 123	49"	Polished Mahogany	30,828.

*For explanation of terms and prices, please see pages 59–65.

Feurich (continued)

Grands

Model	Size	Style and Finish	Price*
F 172	5' 8"	Polished Ebony	67,280.
F 172 ADF	5' 8"	"Old German Style" Polished Ebony	81,600.
F 172 ADF	5' 8"	"Old German Style" Cherry	81,772.
F 172	5' 8"	Rococo	110,323.
F 227	7' 5"	Polished Ebony	100,157.
F 227 ADF	7' 5"	"Old German Style" Polished Ebony	109,674.

Förster, August

Prices do not include bench.

Verticals

Model	Size	Style and Finish	Price*
116C	46"	Chippendale Polished Ebony	19,922.
116C	46"	Chippendale Walnut and Polished Walnut	20,878.
116C	46"	Chippendale Mahog. And Pol. Mahogany	20,004.
116C	46"	Chippendale Polished White	20,373.
116D	46"	Continental Polished Ebony	16,865.
116D	46"	Continental Walnut and Polished Walnut	17,889.
116D	46"	Continental Mahog.and Pol. Mahogany	16,919.
116D	46"	Continental Polished White	17,329.
116E	46"	Polished Ebony	19,922.
116E	46"	Walnut and Polished Walnut	20,878.
116E	46"	Mahogany and Polished Mahogany	20,004.
116E	46"	Polished White	20,373.
125G	49"	Polished Ebony	21,410.
125G	49"	Walnut and Polished Walnut	22,461.
125G	49"	Mahogany and Polished Mahogany	21,479.
125G	49"	Polished White	21,874.

Grands

Model	Size	Style and Finish	Price*
170	5' 8"	Polished Ebony	45,496.
170	5' 8"	Walnut and Polished Walnut	47,134.
170	5' 8"	Mahogany and Polished Mahogany	45,633.
170	5' 8"	Polished White	47,544.
170	5' 8"	*Pyramid Mahogany*	51,775.
170	5' 8"	"Classic" Polished Ebony	50,642.
170	5' 8"	"Classic" Walnut and Polished Walnut	57,440.
170	5' 8"	"Classic" Mahogany and Pol. Mahogany	51,625.
170	5' 8"	"Classic" Polished White	54,614.

Model	Size	Style and Finish	Price*
170	5' 8"	*Chippendale, additional*	10,306.
190	6' 4"	Polished Ebony	51,639.
190	6' 4"	Walnut and Polished Walnut	53,413.
190	6' 4"	Mahogany and Polished Mahogany	51,775.
190	6' 4"	Polished White	53,686.
190	6' 4"	*Pyramid Mahogany*	57,918.
190	6' 4"	"Classic" Polished Ebony	56,785.
190	6' 4"	"Classic" Walnut and Polished Walnut	63,719.
190	6' 4"	"Classic" Mahogany and Pol.Mahogany	57,767.
190	6' 4"	"Classic" Polished White	60,757.
190	6' 4"	*Chippendale, additional*	10,306.
215	7' 2"	Polished Ebony	57,235.
275	9' 1"	Polished Ebony	108,559.

Grotrian

Prices do not include bench. Other woods available on request.

Verticals

Fried. Grotrian	43-1/2"	Polished Ebony	14,320.
Cristal	44"	Polished Ebony	17,242.
Cristal	44"	Open-pore Oak/Walnut	16,846.
Cristal	44"	Polished Walnut/White	18,672.
Carat	45-1/2"	Polished Ebony	21,214.
Carat	45-1/2"	Open-pore Oak/Walnut	20,578.
Carat	45-1/2"	Polished Walnut/White	22,961.
College	48"	Ebony	21,817.
College	48"	Polished Ebony	23,384.
College	48"	Open-pore Beech	21,817.
Classic	49"	Polished Ebony	27,831.
Classic	49"	Open-pore Oak/Walnut	25,847.
Classic	49"	Polished Walnut/White	30,215.
Concertino	52"	Polished Ebony	32,874.
All models		*Sostenuto pedal, add'l*	1,010.

Grands

Chambre	5' 5"	Ebony	48,256.
Chambre	5' 5"	Polished Ebony	53,339.
Chambre	5' 5"	Open-pore Oak/Walnut	49,845.
Chambre	5' 5"	Polished Walnut/White	58,106.
Cabinet	6' 3"	Ebony	54,928.
Cabinet	6' 3"	Polished Ebony	61,442.

*For explanation of terms and prices, please see pages 59–65.

Grotrian (continued)

Cabinet	6' 3"	Open-pore Oak/Walnut	58,106.
Cabinet	6' 3"	Polished Walnut/White	66,206.
Concert	7' 4"	Ebony	71,535.
Concert	7' 4"	Polished Ebony	75,840.
Concert Royal	9' 1"	Polished Ebony	91,941.
All models		*Chippendale/Empire, add'l*	3,003.
All models		*CS Style, add'l*	3,822.
All models		*Rokoko, add'l*	10,784.

Gulbransen

Verticals

87050	45"	Oak	3,390.
87058	45"	Cherry	3,390.
87162	47"	Ebony	3,790.
87170	47"	Mahogany	3,790.

Grands

80462	4' 7"	Ebony	7,500.
80462PM	4' 7"	Ebony w/Pianomation	11,790.
80662	5'	Ebony	8,100.
80662PM	5'	Ebony w/Pianomation	12,590.

Haessler

Prices do not include bench.

Verticals

115 K	45"	Ebony and Polished Ebony	13,180.
115 K	45"	Waxed Alder	12,918.
115 K	45"	Beech	12,918.
115 K	45"	Ash	12,918.
115 K	45"	White and Polished White	13,774.
118 K	47"	Ebony and Polished Ebony	14,744.
118 K	47"	Ebony with Walnut Accent	15,954.
118 K	47"	Mahogany and Polished Mahogany	15,536.
118 K	47"	Walnut and Polished Walnut	15,536.
118 K	47"	Cherry and Polished Cherry	15,976.
118 K	47"	Cherry with Yew Inlay, Satin and Polish	16,856.
118 K	47"	Oak	13,930.

Model	Size	Style and Finish	Price*
118 K	47"	White and Polished White	15,360.
118 KM	47"	Ebony and Polished Ebony	15,624.
118 KM	47"	White and Polished White	16,284.
118 CH	47"	Chippendale Mahogany and Pol.Mahogany	16,856.
118 CH	47"	Chippendale Walnut and Polished Walnut	17,230.
124 K	49"	Ebony and Polished Ebony	15,800.
124 K	49"	Ebony with Walnut Accent	16,702.
124 K	49"	Mahogany and Polished Mahogany	17,120.
124 K	49"	Walnut and Polished Walnut	17,120.
124 K	49"	Cherry and Polished Cherry	17,626.
124 K	49"	Cherry with Yew Inlay, Satin and Polish	18,506.
124 K	49"	White and Polished White	16,460.
124 KM	49"	Ebony and Polished Ebony	16,414.
124 KM	49"	White and Polished White	16,414.
132	52"	Ebony and Polished Ebony	22,242.

Grands

Model	Size	Style and Finish	Price*
175	5' 8"	Ebony and Polished Ebony	46,630.
175	5' 8"	Mahogany and Polished Mahogany	48,495.
175	5' 8"	Walnut and Polished Walnut	48,963.
175	5' 8"	Cherry and Polished Cherry	48,728.
175	5' 8"	Polished Bubinga	51,293.
175	5' 8"	White and Polished White	48,963.
175	5' 8"	Saxony Polished Pyramid Mahogany	61,524.
175	5' 8"	Saxony Polished Burl Walnut	62,115.
175	5' 8"	"President" Polished Ebony	52,059.
175	5' 8"	"President" Polished Mahogany	54,141.
175	5' 8"	"President" Polished Walnut	54,662.
175	5' 8"	"President" Polished Bubinga	57,266.
175	5' 8"	Louis XV, Satin and Polished	54,427.
175	5' 8"	Louis XV Mahogany, Satin and Polished	57,147.
175	5' 8"	Louis XV Walnut, Satin and Polished	56,602.
175	5' 8"	Kaiser Wilhelm II Polished Ebony	54,898.
175	5' 8"	Kaiser Wilhelm II Polished Mahogany	57,093.
175	5' 8"	Kaiser Wilhelm II Polished Walnut	57,645.
175	5' 8"	Kaiser Wilhelm II Polished Cherry	57,369.
175	5' 8"	Ambassador East Indian Rosewood	63,892.
175	5' 8"	Ambassador Walnut	59,159.
175	5' 8"	Nicolas II Walnut w/Burl Inlay	63,892.
175	5' 8"	Louis XVI Rococo White w/Gold	68,624.
175	5' 8"	Classic Alexandra Polished Ebony	53,005.

*For explanation of terms and prices, please see pages 59–65.

Haessler (continued)

Model	Size	Style and Finish	Price
175	5' 8"	Classic Alexandra Polished Mahogany	55,655.
175	5' 8"	Classic Alexandra Polished Walnut	55,124.
186	6' 1"	Ebony and Polished Ebony	52,536.
186	6' 1"	Mahogany and Polished Mahogany	54,310.
186	6' 1"	Walnut and Polished Walnut	55,164.
186	6' 1"	Cherry and Polished Cherry	54,899.
186	6' 1"	Polished Bubinga	57,802.
186	6' 1"	White and Polished White	55,164.
186	6' 1"	Saxony Polished Pyramid Mahogany	69,318.
186	6' 1"	Saxony Polished Burl Walnut	69,983.
186	6' 1"	"President" Polished Ebony	58,654.
186	6' 1"	"President" Polished Mahogany	60,999.
186	6' 1"	"President" Polished Walnut	61,587.
186	6' 1"	"President" Polished Bubinga	64,519.
186	6' 1"	Louis XV, Satin and Polished	61,318.
186	6' 1"	Louis XV Mahogany, Satin and Polished	64,383.
186	6' 1"	Louis XV Walnut, Satin and Polished	63,772.
186	6' 1"	Kaiser Wilhelm II Polished Ebony	61,853.
186	6' 1"	Kaiser Wilhelm II Polished Mahogany	64,327.
186	6' 1"	Kaiser Wilhelm II Polished Walnut	64,945.
186	6' 1"	Kaiser Wilhelm II Polished Cherry	64,636.
186	6' 1"	Ambassador East Indian Rosewood	71,982.
186	6' 1"	Ambassador Walnut	66,652.
186	6' 1"	Nicolas II Walnut w/Burl Inlay	71,982.
186	6' 1"	Louis XVI Rococo White w/Gold	77,316.
186	6' 1"	Classic Alexandra Polished Ebony	59,720.
186	6' 1"	Classic Alexandra Polished Mahogany	62,706.
186	6' 1"	Classic Alexandra Polished Walnut	62,108.

Hallet, Davis & Co.

Verticals

Model	Size	Style and Finish	Price
H-C43F	43"	French Oak	2,990.
H-C43F	43"	French Mahogany	2,990.
H-C43F	43"	French Cherry	2,990.
H-C43F	43"	French Walnut	2,990.
H-C43R	43"	Oak (round leg)	2,990.
H-C43R	43"	Mahogany (round leg)	2,990.
H-C43S	43"	Italian Provincial Walnut	2,990.

Model	Size	Style and Finish	Price*
H-C43S	43"	Italian Provincial Mahogany	2,990.
H-C43S	43"	Italian Provincial Cherry	2,990.
H-111GD	44"	Continental Polished Ebony	2,500.
H-111GD	44"	Continental Polished Mahogany	2,550.
H-111GD	44"	Continental Polished Walnut	2,550.
H-111GD	44"	Continental Polished White	2,550.
H-115GC	45"	Chippendale Polished Ebony	2,750.
H-115GC	45"	Chippendale Polished Mahogany	2,790.
H-115WH	46"	Polished Ebony	2,790.
H-115WH	46"	Polished Mahogany	2,840.
H-115WH	46"	Polished Walnut	2,840.
H-121WH	48"	Polished Ebony	2,990.
H-121WH	48"	Polished Mahogany	3,100.
H-121WH	48"	Polished Walnut	3,100.
H-126	50"	Polished Ebony	3,590.
H-126	50"	Polished Mahogany	3,700.

Grands

Model	Size	Style and Finish	Price*
H-143	4' 8"	Polished Ebony	6,390.
H-143	4' 8"	Polished Mahogany	6,790.
H-143	4' 8"	Polished Walnut	6,790.
H-143F	4' 8"	Queen Anne Polished Ebony	7,190.
H-143F	4' 8"	Queen Anne Polished Mahogany	7,190.
H-143F	4' 8"	Queen Anne Polished Walnut	7,190.
H-152C	5'	Ebony	8,390.
H-152C	5'	Polished Ebony	7,990.
H-152C	5'	Mahogany	8,590.
H-152C	5'	Polished Mahogany	8,390.
H-152C	5'	Polished Walnut	8,390.
H-152C	5'	Polished White	8,390.
H-152D	5'	Polished Ebony	8,590.
H-152D	5'	Mahogany	9,190.
H-152D	5'	Polished Mahogany	8,990.
H-152D	5'	Polished Walnut	8,990.
H-152S	5'	Queen Anne Polished Ebony	8,590.
H-152S	5'	Queen Anne Mahogany	9,190.
H-152S	5'	Queen Anne Polished Mahogany	8,990.
H-165C	5' 5"	Ebony	9,190.
H-165C	5' 5"	Polished Ebony	8,790.
H-165C	5' 5"	Mahogany	9,390.

*For explanation of terms and prices, please see pages 59–65.

Model	Size	Style and Finish	Price*

Hallet, Davis & Co. (continued)

Model	Size	Style and Finish	Price*
H-165C	5' 5"	Polished Mahogany	9,190.
H-165C	5' 5"	Polished Walnut	9,190.
H-165C	5' 5"	Polished White	9,190.
H-165D	5' 5"	Polished Mahogany	9,790.
H-185C	6' 1"	Polished Ebony	10,790.
H-185C	6' 1"	Polished Mahogany	11,190.
H-185C	6' 1"	Polished Walnut	11,190.
H-215C	7' 1"	Polished Ebony	16,990.

Hamilton

Verticals

Model	Size	Style and Finish	Price
W-H100	39"	Continental Polished Ebony (73-note)	1,978.
W-H100	39"	Continental Polished Cherry (73-note)	2,098.
W-H350	42-1/2"	Continental Polished Ebony	2,790.
W-H350	42-1/2"	Continental Polished Mahogany	2,790.
W-H310	44"	Vintage Mahogany	2,990.
W-H310	44"	American Oak	2,990.
W-H310	44"	Royal Cherry	2,990.
W-H360	47"	Classic Polished Ebony	3,390.
W-H360	47"	Classic Polished Mahogany	3,390.

Grands

Model	Size	Style and Finish	Price
W-H391	4' 7"	Polished Ebony	7,750.
W-H391	4' 7"	Polished Mahogany	7,950.
W-H391	4' 7"	Polished White	7,750.
W-H396	5' 1"	Polished Ebony	8,990.
W-H396	5' 1"	Polished Mahogany	9,290.
W-H396	5' 1"	Polished White	8,990.
W-H398	5' 4"	Polished Ebony	10,050.
W-H398	5' 4"	Polished Mahogany	10,050.
W-H399	5' 8"	Ebony	10,798.
W-H399	5' 8"	Polished Ebony	10,398.
W-H399	5' 8"	Polished Mahogany	10,798.
W-H401	6' 2"	Polished Ebony	11,500.
W-H401	6' 2"	Polished Mahogany	11,500.

Ibach

Verticals

Model	Size	Style and Finish	Price*
B-114	45"	"Classic/Tradition" Open-Pore Beech	16,754.
B-114	45"	"Classic/Tradition" Open-Pore Alder	16,754.
B-114	45"	"Classic/Tradition" Open-Pore Oak	16,754.
B-114	45"	"Classic/Tradition" Open-Pore Maple	17,115.
B-114	45"	"Classic/Tradition" Open-Pore Cherry	17,115.
C-118	46-1/2"	"Elegance" Open-Pore Beech	18,054.
C-118	46-1/2"	"Elegance" Open-Pore Oak	18,054.
C-118	46-1/2"	"Elegance" Open-Pore Cherry	18,460.
C-118	46-1/2"	"Elegance" Polished Ebony	18,517.
C-118	46-1/2"	"Elegance" Polished White	19,155.
C-118	46-1/2"	"Elegance" Polished Walnut	19,910.
C-118	46-1/2"	"Elegance" Polished Mahogany	19,910.
C-118	46-1/2"	"Elegance" Polished Cherry	19,910.
C-118	46-1/2"	"Elegance" Polished Burr Walnut	22,057.
C-118	46-1/2"	"Edition (Bruno Paul 1911)" Pol. Ebony	21,651.
C-118	46-1/2"	"Edition (Bruno Paul 1911)" Pol. White	22,436.
C-118	46-1/2"	"Edition (Bruno Paul 1911)" Oiled Oak	22,436.
C-118	46-1/2"	"Antik" Polished Ebony	on request
K-125	49"	"Exclusive" Polished Ebony	on request
H-128	50"	"Edition" Swiss Pear-Tree	on request
L-132	52"	"Tradition" Polished Ebony	26,060.

Grands

Model	Size	Style and Finish	Price*
F-II 183	6'	Polished Ebony	53,731.
F-II 183	6'	Polished Mahogany	59,474.
F-II 183	6'	Polished Burr Walnut	60,912.
F-II 183	6'	*"Edition Ibach Design 1913"*	56,318.
F-II 183	6'	*"Eigenentwurf Ibach Design 1908"*	55,680.
F-II 183	6'	*"Ausfuhrung Art Design"*	66,873.
F-III 215	7' 1"	"Richard Strauss" Polished Ebony	68,064.
F-III 215	7' 1"	*"Klassizismus"*	115,767.
F-III 215	7' 1"	*"Richard Meier"*	on request
F-IV 240	7' 10-1/2"	"Richard Wagner" Polished Ebony	74,168.

Irmler

Verticals

Model	Size	Style and Finish	Price*
M113E	44"	Polished Ebony	7,611.

*For explanation of terms and prices, please see pages 59–65.

Irmler (continued)

Model	Size	Style and Finish	Price*
M113E	44"	Walnut/Beech/Alder	7,361.
M113E	44"	Mahogany/Cherry	7,540.
M113E	44"	Polished Walnut/Mahogany/Cherry	7,730.
M113E	44"	Polished White	8,090.
M122E	49"	Polished Ebony	8,149.
M122E	49"	Walnut	7,910.
M122E	49"	Mahogany/Cherry	8,090.
M122E	49"	Beech/Alder	7,730.
M122E	49"	Polished Walnut	8,090.
M122E	49"	Polished Mahogany/Cherry	8,279.
M122E	49"	Polished Cherry with Inlay	8,989.
M122E	49"	Polished Bubinga	9,710.
M122E	49"	Polished White	8,640.

Grands

Model	Size	Style and Finish	Price*
F16E	5' 7"	Polished Ebony	27,321.
F16E	5' 7"	Walnut/Mahogany	28,249.
F16E	5' 7"	Cherry	27,369.
F16E	5' 7"	Polished Walnut/Mahogany	28,960.
F16E	5' 7"	Polished Cherry	29,570.
F16E	5' 7"	Polished White	28,010.
F18E	6' 1"	Polished Ebony	29,340.
F18E	6' 1"	Walnut/Mahogany	30,310.
F18E	6' 1"	Cherry	29,640.
F18E	6' 1"	Polished Walnut	30,949.
F18E	6' 1"	Polished Mahogany	30,981.
F18E	6' 1"	Polished Cherry	31,621.
F18E	6' 1"	Polished White	30,701.
F18E	6' 1"	"Classic" Polished Ebony	34,589.
F18E	6' 1"	"Classic" Polished Walnut/Mahogany	35,900.
F18E	6' 1"	"Classic" Polished Cherry	36,569.
F18E	6' 1"	Chippendale Polished Ebony	34,589.
F18E	6' 1"	Chippendale Polished Walnut/Mahogany	36,220.
F18E	6' 1"	Chippendale Polished White	36,220.
F22E	7' 3"	Polished Ebony	42,671.
F22E	7' 3"	Polished Walnut/Mahogany/Cherry	45,810.
F22E	7' 3"	Polished White	44,759.

Kawai

Verticals

Model	Size	Style and Finish	Price*
K-18	44-1/2"	Polished Ebony	4,730.
K-18	44-1/2"	Polished Mahogany	5,330.
506N	44-1/2"	Mahogany/Oak	3,590.
508	44-1/2"	Mahogany/Oak	4,190.
606	44-1/2"	American Oak	4,490.
606	45"	Spanish Provincial Oak	5,890.
608	44-1/2"	Classic Spanish Oak	5,090.
608	44-1/2"	French Provincial Cherry	5,190.
608	44-1/2"	Queen Anne Mahogany	5,190.
UST-7	46"	Ebony/Oak/Walnut	6,690.
UST-8	46"	Ebony/Oak/Walnut	5,590.
906	46-1/2"	English Regency Mahogany	7,190.
906	46-1/2"	French Provincial Cherry	7,190.
UST-10	48"	Ebony/Mahogany	7,990.
K-25	48"	Ebony and Polished Ebony	5,790.
K-25	48"	Mahogany and Polished Mahogany	6,390.
K-25	48"	Polished Snow White	6,190.
K-50	49"	Ebony and Polished Ebony	7,990.
K-50	49"	Polished Sapeli Mahogany	9,290.
K-50	49"	Walnut	8,890.
K-50	49"	Polished Walnut	9,290.
UST-12	52"	Ebony/Mahogany	9,990.
K-60	52"	Ebony and Polished Ebony	10,790.
K-80	52"	Ebony and Polished Ebony	12,990.
VT-132	52"	Vari-Touch Polished Ebony	11,590.

Grands

Model	Size	Style and Finish	Price*
GM-10LE	5'	Ebony and Polished Ebony	12,390.
GM-10LE	5'	Polished Mahogany/Snow White	13,590.
GE-20	5' 1"	Ebony and Polished Ebony	14,890.
GE-20	5' 1"	Walnut	16,390.
GE-20	5' 1"	Mahogany	16,190.
GE-20	5' 1"	Polished Mahogany	16,590.
GE-20	5' 1"	Polished Sapeli Mahogany	16,590.
GE-20	5' 1"	Polished Snow White	15,990.
GE-20	5' 1"	French Provincial Polished Mahogany	17,990.
GE-20C	5' 1"	Conservatory Polished Ebony	14,890.
GE-30	5' 5"	Ebony and Polished Ebony	16,990.

*For explanation of terms and prices, please see pages 59–65.

Kawai (continued)

Model	Size	Style and Finish	Price*
GE-30	5' 5"	Mahogany	18,890.
GE-30	5' 5"	Walnut	18,690.
GE-30	5' 5"	Polished Mahogany	18,990.
GE-30	5' 5"	Polished Sapeli Mahogany	18,890.
GE-30	5' 5"	Polished Snow White	18,190.
GE-30C	5' 5"	Conservatory Polished Ebony	16,990.
RX-1	5' 5"	Ebony and Polished Ebony	19,990.
RX-1	5' 5"	Walnut	21,390.
RX-1	5' 5"	Polished Walnut	21,990.
RX-1	5' 5"	Polished Sapeli Mahogany	21,590.
RX-1	5' 5"	Polished Snow White	20,790.
RX-2	5' 10"	Ebony and Polished Ebony	22,690.
RX-2	5' 10"	Walnut/Cherry	24,390.
RX-2	5' 10"	Polished Walnut	25,590.
RX-2	5' 10"	Polished Mahogany	24,390.
RX-2	5' 10"	Polished Sapeli Mahogany	24,590.
RX-2	5' 10"	Oak	23,390.
RX-2	5' 10"	Polished Rosewood	28,990.
RX-2	5' 10"	Polished Snow White	23,790.
RX-2	5' 10"	French Provincial Polished Mahogany	28,790.
RX-3	6' 1"	Ebony and Polished Ebony	29,390.
RX-3	6' 1"	Walnut	31,590.
RX-3	6' 1"	Polished Sapeli Mahogany	32,190.
RX-3	6' 1"	Polished Snow White	30,390.
CR40N	6' 1"	Plexiglass	75,260.
RX-5	6' 6"	Ebony and Polished Ebony	32,790.
RX-5	6' 6"	Walnut	35,690.
RX-5	6' 6"	Polished Sapeli Mahogany	35,690.
RX-5	6' 6"	Polished Snow White	34,190.
RX-6	7'	Ebony and Polished Ebony	36,790.
RX-7	7' 6"	Ebony and Polished Ebony	42,190.
GS-100	9' 1"	Polished Ebony	79,990.
EX	9' 1"	Polished Ebony	109,190.
EX-G	9' 1"	Polished Ebony	115,990.

Kawai, Shigeru

Grands

Model	Size	Style and Finish	Price*
SK2	5' 10"	Polished Ebony	36,700.

Model	Size	Style and Finish	Price*
SK2	5' 10"	Polished Sapeli Mahogany	38,700.
SK2	5' 10"	Polished Pyramid Mahogany	58,700.
SK2	5' 10"	"Classic Noblesse" w/Burl Walnut Inlay	56,500.
SK3	6' 1"	Polished Ebony	42,900.
SK3	6' 1"	Polished Sapeli Mahogany	45,300.
SK5	6' 6"	Polished Ebony	49,300.
SK5	6' 6"	Polished Sapeli Mahogany	52,300.
SK6	7'	Polished Ebony	55,700.
SK7	7' 6"	Polished Ebony	61,700.
SK7	7' 6"	Polished Pyramid Mahogany	93,300.
SK7	7' 6"	"Classic Noblesse" w/Burl Walnut Inlay	84,900.

Kemble

Verticals

Cambridge 10	43"	Mahogany/Walnut	7,040.
Oxford	43"	Mahogany/Walnut	7,240.
Oxford	43"	Mahogany with Inlay	7,660.
Classic-T	45"	Polished Ebony	8,400.
Classic-T	45"	Polished Ebony and Chrome	8,700.
Empire	46-1/2"	Empire Polished Mahogany	10,240.
Prestige	46-1/2"	Cherry with Yew Inlay	10,240.
Windsor	46-1/2"	Polished Ebony with Burr Walnut	9,340.
Windsor	46-1/2"	Polished Mahogany	9,140.
K121ZT	48"	Polished Ebony	10,240.
K121ZT	48"	Polished Mahogany/Walnut	10,240.
K121ZT	48"	Georgian Mahogany Lustre	9,990.
Vermont	48"	Cherry	11,940.
Quantum II	49"	Polished Ebony	11,940.
K131	52"	Polished Ebony	13,640.
K131	52"	Polished Mahogany	13,640.
K131	52"	Walnut	12,740.

Grands

KC 173	5' 8"	Polished Ebony	24,990.

Kimball

Grands

K1	4' 10"	Polished Ebony	7,390.
K1	4' 10"	Polished Mahogany	7,790.

*For explanation of terms and prices, please see pages 59–65.

Knabe, Wm.

Verticals

Model	Size	Style and Finish	Price*
WKV-118F	46-1/2"	Fr. Provincial Polished Mahog./Cherry	5,990.
WKV-118R	46-1/2"	Renaissance Polished Ebony/Walnut	5,990.
WKV-118R	46-1/2"	Renaissance Oak	5,490.
WKV-118T	46-1/2"	Polished Mahogany/Walnut/Cherry	5,990.
WKV-121D	48"	Ebony	6,190.
WKV-121D	48"	Polished Ebony	5,990.
WKV-131MD	52"	Ebony	6,390.
WKV-131MD	52"	Polished Ebony	6,190.

Grands

Model	Size	Style and Finish	Price*
WKG-53	5' 3"	Ebony	14,390.
WKG-53	5' 3"	Polished Ebony	13,990.
WKG-53	5' 3"	Semi-Gloss Mahogany/Walnut/Cherry	14,990.
WKG-53KBF	5' 3"	Fr. Prov. Semi-Gloss Mahog./Wal./Cherry	17,990.
WKG-53M	5' 3"	Empire Ebony	16,990.
WKG-53M	5' 3"	Empire Polished Ebony	16,590.
WKG-53M	5' 3"	Empire Semi-Gloss Mahog./Walnut/Cherry	17,990.
WKG-57	5' 7"	Ebony	18,390.
WKG-57	5' 7"	Polished Ebony	17,990.
WKG-57	5' 7"	Semi-Gloss Mahogany/Walnut/Cherry	19,390.
WKG-58	5' 8"	Ebony	19,390.
WKG-58	5' 8"	Polished Ebony	18,990.
WKG-58	5' 8"	Semi-Gloss Mahogany/Walnut/Cherry	20,390.
WKG-58F	5' 8"	Louis XV Semi-Gloss Mahogany/Walnut	21,990.
WKG-58M	5' 8"	Empire Ebony	20,390.
WKG-58M	5' 8"	Empire Polished Ebony	19,590.
WKG-58M	5' 8"	Empire Semi-Gloss Mahog./Walnut/Cherry	21,190.
WKG-61	6' 1"	Ebony and Polished Ebony	20,200.
WKG-61	6' 1"	Semi-Gloss Mahogany/Walnut/Cherry	21,200.
WKG-61L	6' 1"	Empire Semi-Gloss Mahog./Walnut/Cherry	23,000.
WKG-64	6' 4"	Ebony	20,990.
WKG-64	6' 4"	Semi-Gloss Mahogany/Walnut	21,990.
WKG-70	7'	Ebony and Polished Ebony	23,800.

Kohler & Campbell

Verticals

Model	Size	Style and Finish	Price*
KC-142	42"	Continental Polished Ebony	2,750.

Model	Size	Style and Finish	Price*
KC-142	42"	Continental Cherry/Walnut	2,850.
KC-142	42"	Continental Polished Mahogany/Walnut	2,850.
KC-142	42"	Continental Polished Ivory	2,850.
KC-244F	44"	French Provincial Cherry	3,590.
KC-244M	44"	Mediterranean Brown Oak	3,590.
KC-244T	44"	Mahogany	3,590.
KC-245	45"	Ebony and Polished Ebony	3,190.
KC-245	45"	Mahogany/Cherry/Walnut	3,190.
KC-245	45"	Polished Mahogany	3,190.
KC-247	46-1/2"	Ebony and Polished Ebony	4,700.
KC-247	46-1/2"	Mahogany/Brown Oak/Walnut	4,700.
KC-247	46-1/2"	Polished Mahogany/Walnut	4,700.
KC-647F	46-1/2"	French Provincial Cherry	4,190.
KC-647R	46-1/2"	Renaissance Walnut	3,990.
KC-647T	46-1/2"	Mahogany	4,190.
KMV-47F	46-1/2"	Fr. Provincial Semi-gloss Cherry/Mahogany	5,500.
KMV-47T	46-1/2"	Semi-gloss Cherry/Mahogany	5,500.
KMV-47T	46-1/2"	American Oak	5,310.
KC-121F	48"	French Provincial Polished Ebony	4,190.
KC-121F	48"	French Provincial Polished Mahogany	4,390.
KC-121M	48"	Mediterranean Polished Ebony	3,990.
KC-121M	48"	Mediterranean Polished Mahogany	4,270.
KMV-48SD	48"	Ebony	7,090.
KMV-48SD	48"	Polished Ebony	5,690.
KMV-48SD	48"	Polished Mahogany	7,090.
KC-131	52"	Polished Ebony	3,990.
KMV-52MD	52"	Ebony	7,470.
KMV-52MD	52"	Polished Ebony	6,070.
KMV-52MD	52"	Polished Mahogany	7,470.

Grands

Model	Size	Style and Finish	Price*
KCG-450	4' 9"	Ebony	8,590.
KCG-450	4' 9"	Polished Ebony	8,390.
KCG-450	4' 9"	Polished Mahogany	8,990.
KCG-450KBF	4' 9"	French Provincial Pol. Mahogany/Cherry	10,390.
KCG-500	5' 1-1/2"	Ebony	9,990.
KCG-500	5' 1-1/2"	Polished Ebony	9,790.
KCG-500	5' 1-1/2"	Polished Mahogany	10,390.
KCG-500KBF	5' 1-1/2"	French Provincial Pol. Mahogany/Cherry	11,790.
SKG-530S	5' 2"	Ebony	11,990.
SKG-530S	5' 2"	Polished Ebony	11,590.

*For explanation of terms and prices, please see pages 59–65.

Model	Size	Style and Finish	Price*

Kohler & Campbell (continued)

Model	Size	Style and Finish	Price*
SKG-530S	5' 2"	Polished Mahogany	12,990.
KFM-530A	5' 2"	Ebony	13,390.
KFM-530A	5' 2"	Polished Ebony	12,990.
KFM-530A	5' 2"	Polished Mahogany	14,390.
KFM-530M	5' 2"	Empire Ebony	14,590.
KFM-530M	5' 2"	Empire Polished Ebony	14,190.
KFM-530M	5' 2"	Empire Polished Mahogany	15,590.
KFM-530AKBF	5' 2"	French Provincial Polished Mahogany	16,390.
KCG-600	5' 9"	Ebony	10,990.
KCG-600	5' 9"	Polished Ebony	10,790.
KCG-600	5' 9"	Polished Mahogany	11,390.
KCG-600L	5' 9"	Empire Polished Ebony	11,990.
KCG-600L	5' 9"	Empire Polished Mahogany	12,590.
KFM-600A	5' 9"	Ebony	16,390.
KFM-600A	5' 9"	Polished Ebony	15,990.
KFM-600A	5' 9"	Polished Mahogany	17,390.
KCG-650	6' 1"	Ebony	11,790.
KCG-650	6' 1"	Polished Ebony	11,590.
KCG-650	6' 1"	Polished Mahogany	12,190.
KFM-650A	6' 1"	Ebony	17,590.
KFM-650A	6' 1"	Polished Ebony	17,190.
KFM-650A	6' 1"	Polished Mahogany	18,590.
KFM-650L	6' 1"	Empire Polished Mahogany	21,990.
KFM-700A	6' 8"	Polished Ebony	23,000.

Mason & Hamlin

Verticals

Model	Size	Style and Finish	Price*
50	50"	Polished Ebony	17,862.

Grands

Model	Size	Style and Finish	Price*
A	5' 8"	Ebony	45,368.
A	5' 8"	Polished Ebony	48,516.
A	5' 8"	Mahogany/Walnut	48,780.
A	5' 8"	Polished Pyramid Mahogany	59,298.
A	5' 8"	Rosewood	54,144.
A	5' 8"	Polished Bubinga	56,038.
A	5' 8"	Polished Macassar Ebony	59,298.
A	5' 8"	"Monticello" Polished Ebony	51,682.

Model	Size	Style and Finish	Price*
A	5' 8"	"Monticello" Mahogany	51,930.
A	5' 8"	"Monticello" Rosewood	62,954.
AA	6' 4"	Ebony	52,344.
AA	6' 4"	Polished Ebony	54,042.
AA	6' 4"	Mahogany	55,100.
BB	7'	Ebony	59,322.
BB	7'	Polished Ebony	61,028.
BB	7'	Mahogany/Walnut	61,422.
BB	7'	Polished Pyramid Mahogany	73,130.
BB	7'	Rosewood	68,758.
BB	7'	Polished Bubinga	70,464.
BB	7'	Polished Macassar Ebony	73,130.
BB	7'	"Monticello" Polished Ebony	63,942.
BB	7'	"Monticello" Mahogany	64,572.
BB	7'	"Monticello" Rosewood	79,246.
CC	9' 4"	Ebony	88,200.
CC	9' 4"	Polished Ebony	92,200.

McPhail

Verticals

	44"	Console w/toeblock Ebony Polish/Satin	3,190.
	44"	Console w/toeblock Mahogany	3,289.
	44"	Console w/toeblock Furniture Cabinet	3,454.
	47"	Studio w/toeblock Ebony Polish/Satin	3,738.
	47"	Studio w/toeblock Mahogany	3,888.
	47"	Studio w/toeblock Furniture Cabinet	4,288.

Grands

	5'	Ebony and Polished Ebony	8,327.
	5'	Mahogany	8,723.
	5' 4"	Ebony and Polished Ebony	9,280.
	5' 4"	Mahogany	9,825.

Miller, Henry F.

Verticals

HMV-043	42-1/2"	Continental Polished Ebony	3,200.
HMV-043	42-1/2"	Continental Polished Mahogany	3,350.
HMV-045	43"	French Provincial Polished Cherry	4,220.
HMV-045	43"	Polished Oak/Cherry	4,220.

*For explanation of terms and prices, please see pages 59–65.

Miller, Henry F. (continued)

Model	Size	Style and Finish	Price
HMV-047	46"	Polished Ebony	3,800.
HMV-047	46"	Polished Mahogany	4,000.
HMV-048	48"	Cherry	4,720.

Grands

Model	Size	Style and Finish	Price
HMG-056	4' 7"	Polished Ebony	9,070.
HMG-056	4' 7"	Polished Mahogany	9,120.
HMG-056F	4' 7"	French Provincial Cherry	9,920.
HMG-063	5' 3"	Ebony	10,530.
HMG-063	5' 3"	Polished Ebony	10,330.
HMG-063	5' 3"	Polished Mahogany	10,730.
HMG-063F	5' 3"	French Provincial Cherry	11,730.
HMG-072	6'	Ebony	14,340.
HMG-072	6'	Polished Ebony	14,140.
HMG-072	6'	Polished Mahogany	14,540.

Nordiska

Verticals

Model	Size	Style and Finish	Price
109-CM	43"	Continental Polished Ebony/Mahogany	2,480.
114-MC	45"	French Walnut/Mahogany	3,580.
114-MCH	45"	Walnut/Mahogany	3,580.
116-CB	46"	Chippendale Polished Ebony	3,580.
116-CB	46"	Chippendale Polished Walnut/Mahogany	3,580.
116-MC	46"	Polished Ebony	3,580.
116-MC	46"	Walnut	3,580.
118-C GT	48"	Polished Ebony	3,480.
118-MC	48"	Walnut/Mahogany/Oak	3,780.
120-CA	48"	Polished Ebony/Mahogany	3,780.
126-Pro	50"	Polished Ebony	4,580.
126-Pro	50"	Walnut	4,580.

Grands

Model	Size	Style and Finish	Price
152-C	5'	Polished Ebony	7,980.
152-C	5'	Walnut	8,380.
152-C	5'	Polished Sapeli Mahogany	8,380.
152-C	5'	Polished White	8,380.
152-C I	5'	Polished Walnut/Mahogany	8,580.
152-DC	5'	Demi-Chippendale Polished Ebony	8,900.
152-DC I	5'	Demi-Chippendale Pol. Mahogany/Walnut	9,380.

Model	Size	Style and Finish	Price*
165-CM	5' 5"	Polished Ebony	9,180.
165-CM	5' 5"	Polished Sapeli Mahogany	9,500.
165-CM I	5' 5"	Polished Walnut/Mahogany	9,700.
165-DC	5' 5"	Demi-Chippendale Polished Ebony	10,180.
165-DC I	5' 5"	Demi-Chippendale Pol. Mahogany/Walnut	10,700.
165-R	5' 5"	Regency Polished Ebony	9,780.
165-R I	5' 5"	Regency Polished Mahogany/Walnut	10,300.
185-C	6' 1"	Polished Ebony	10,980.
185-C I	6' 1"	Polished Mahogany/Walnut	11,500.
185-I	6' 1"	Imperial Polished Ebony	11,580.
185-I I	6' 1"	Imperial Polished Mahogany/Walnut	12,100.
185-M	6' 1"	Polished Ebony	11,780.
185-M	6' 1"	Polished Mahogany/Walnut	12,300.
185-PN	6' 1"	Polished Ebony	11,380.
215	7'	Polished Ebony	19,980.
275	9'	Polished Ebony	51,800.

Palatino

Verticals

Model	Size	Style and Finish	Price*
PUP-110T	43-1/2"	Continental Polished Ebony	2,767.
PUP-110T	43-1/2"	Continental Polished Mahogany	2,933.
PUP-110T	43-1/2"	Continental Polished White	2,933.
PUP-123C	48-1/2"	Mahogany	3,650.
PUP-123T	48-1/2"	Ebony	4,123.
PUP-123T	48-1/2"	Polished Ebony	3,650.
PUP-123T	48-1/2"	Mahogany and Polished Mahogany	3,483.
PUP-123T	48-1/2"	Red	3,517.
PUP-123T	48-1/2"	Polished White	3,623.
PUP-126	50"	Ebony and Polished Ebony	3,983.
PUP-126	50"	Polished Mahogany	4,150.

Most vertical models available with slow-close fallboard for an add'l 140.

*For explanation of terms and prices, please see pages 59–65.

Palatino (continued)

Grands

Model	Size	Style and Finish	Price*
PGD-49	4' 9"	Polished Ebony	9,667.
PGD-49	4' 9"	Red	9,900.
PGD-50	5'	Polished Ebony	9,983.
PGD-50	5'	Polished Mahogany	10,217.
PGD-50	5'	Red	10,217.
PGD-50	5'	Polished White	10,217.
PGD-55	5' 5"	Ebony and Polished Ebony	10,650.
PGD-55	5' 5"	Polished Mahogany	10,883.
PGD-55	5' 5"	Polished White	10,883.
PGD-59	5' 9"	Polished Ebony	12,650.

Pearl River

Verticals

Model	Size	Style and Finish	Price*
UP-108D3	42-1/2"	Continental Polished Ebony	2,640.
UP-108D3	42-1/2"	Continental Polished Mahogany/Walnut	2,730.
UP-108D3	42-1/2"	Continental Polished White	2,730.
UP-108M2	42-1/2"	Demi-Chippendale Polished Ebony	3,130.
UP-108M2	42-1/2"	Demi-Chippendale Pol. Mahogany/Walnut	3,180.
UP-108T2	44"	Polished Ebony	3,380.
UP-108T2	44"	Polished Mahogany/Walnut	3,440.
UP-108T2	44"	Polished White	3,530.
UP-110P1	43-1/2"	Walnut/Cherry/Oak	3,710.
UP-110P2	43-1/2"	French Provincial Oak	3,780.
UP-110P2	43-1/2"	French Provincial Cherry	3,900.
UP-110P5	43-1/2"	Italian Provincial Walnut/Cherry	3,970.
UP-110P6	43-1/2"	French Classic Cherry	4,040.
UP-115E	45"	Ebony/Oak/Walnut	3,390.
UP-115M	45"	Polished Ebony	3,230.
UP-115M	45"	Polished Dark Mahogany	3,270.
UP-115P1	45"	Walnut/Cherry	4,280.
UP-118E	47"	Polished Ebony	3,550.
UP-118E	47"	Polished Mahogany/Walnut	3,630.
UP-118E	47"	Polished White	3,630.
UP-120S	48"	Polished Ebony	4,150.
UP-120S	48"	Polished Mahogany	4,250.
UP-125M1	49"	Polished Ebony (with Yamaha)	5,140.
UP-130T2	51-1/2"	Polished Mahogany w/Burl Oval Inlay	5,480.

Model	Size	Style and Finish	Price*
Grands			
GP-142	4' 7"	Polished Ebony	7,860.
GP-142	4' 7"	Polished Mahogany/Walnut	8,380.
GP-142	4' 7"	Polished White	8,380.
GP-142D	4' 7"	French Provincial Cherry	8,910.
GP-142P	4' 7"	Walnut	9,260.
GP-150	5'	Ebony	8,820.
GP-150	5'	Polished Ebony	8,500.
GP-150	5'	Cherry	8,820.
GP-150D	5'	Designer Cherry	9,540.
GP-159	5' 3"	Ebony	11,350.
GP-159	5' 3"	Polished Ebony	11,020.
GP-159	5' 3"	Mahogany and Polished Mahogany	11,350.
GP-170	5' 7"	Ebony	14,070.
GP-170	5' 7"	Polished Ebony	13,710.
GP-170	5' 7"	Mahogany	14,270.
GP-170	5' 7"	Polished Mahogany	13,910.
GP-170D	5' 7"	French Provincial Cherry	14,400.
GP-183	6'	Polished Ebony	14,600.
GP-186	6' 1"	Polished Ebony (Silver Plate & Trim)	15,730.
GP-188	6' 4"	Polished Ebony	17,530.
GP-213	7'	Polished Ebony	20,530.
GP-275	9'	Polished Ebony	55,500.

Perzina, Gebr.

Model	Size	Style and Finish	Price*
Verticals			
GP-112	44"	Continental Polished Ebony	4,990.
GP-112	44"	Continental Pol. Mahogany/Walnut/Oak	5,190.
GP-112	44"	Continental Polished White	5,190.
GP-112	44"	Continental Satin Finishes	5,190.
GP-112	44"	Polished Ebony	5,190.
GP-112	44"	Polished Mahogany/Walnut/Oak	5,380.
GP-112	44"	Polished White	5,380.
GP-112	44"	Satin Finishes	5,380.
GP-112	44"	Queen Anne Polished Ebony	5,380.
GP-112	44"	Queen Anne Polished Mahogany/Walnut	5,580.
GP-112	44"	Queen Anne Walnut	5,580.
GP-118	46-1/2"	Continental Polished Ebony	5,980.

*For explanation of terms and prices, please see pages 59–65.

Perzina, Gebr. (continued)

Model	Size	Style and Finish	Price*
GP-118	46-1/2"	Continental Pol. Ebony w/Mahog. Center	6,220.
GP-118	46-1/2"	Continental Pol. Mahogany/Walnut/Oak	6,280.
GP-118	46-1/2"	Continental Polished White	6,280.
GP-118	46-1/2"	Continental Satin Finishes	6,280.
GP-118	46-1/2"	Walnut/Mahogany/Oak	6,880.
GP-118	46-1/2"	Contemporary Walnut/Mahogany/Oak	6,880.
GP-118	46-1/2"	Queen Anne Walnut/Mahogany/Oak	6,880.
GP-118	46-1/2"	Country French Mahogany/Oak	6,880.
GP-122	48"	Polished Ebony	6,890.
GP-122	48"	Polished Ebony with Pommele Center	7,120.
GP-122	48"	Polished Mahogany/Walnut/Oak	7,190.
GP-122	48"	Polished White	7,190.
GP-122	48"	Satin Finishes	7,190.
GP-122	48"	Deco Leg Polished Ebony	7,140.
GP-122	48"	Deco Leg Polished Ebony w/Walnut Trim	7,440.
GP-122	48"	Deco Leg Polished Mahogany/Oak	7,440.
GP-122	48"	Deco Leg Polished White	7,440.
GP-122	48"	Queen Anne Polished Ebony	7,140.
GP-122	48"	Queen Anne Polished Mahogany/Walnut	7,440.
GP-122	48"	Queen Anne Walnut	7,440.
GP-126	49"	Queen Anne Polished Ebony w/molding	7,290.
GP-126	49"	Queen Anne Polished Mahogany w/molding	7,640.
GP-126	49"	Queen Anne Polished Walnut w/molding	7,640.
GP-126	49"	Queen Anne Walnut w/molding	7,640.
GP-129	51"	Polished Ebony	7,790.
GP-129	51"	Polished Ebony w/Pommele Center	8,020.
GP-129	51"	Polished Mahogany/Walnut/Oak	8,290.
GP-129	51"	Polished White	8,290.
GP-129	51"	Satin Finishes	8,290.
GP-129	51"	Queen Anne Polished Ebony	8,020.
GP-129	51"	Queen Anne Polished Mahogany/Walnut	8,530.
GP-129	51"	Queen Anne Walnut	8,530.
GP-129	51"	Queen Anne Polished Ebony w/molding	8,180.
GP-129	51"	Queen Anne Polished Mahogany w/molding	8,760.
GP-129	51"	Queen Anne Polished Walnut w/molding	8,760.
GP-129	51"	Queen Anne Walnut w/molding	8,760.

Grands

Model	Size	Style and Finish	Price*
E-160	5' 3"	Polished Ebony	22,990.
E-160	5' 3"	Polished Mahogany/Walnut	24,390.

Model	Size	Style and Finish	Price*
G-160	5' 3"	Polished Ebony	15,990.
G-160	5' 3"	Polished Mahogany/Walnut/Oak	16,490.
G-160	5' 3"	Polished White	16,490.
G-160	5' 3"	Satin Finishes	16,490.
G-160	5' 3"	Polished Ebony (round leg)	16,190.
G-160	5' 3"	Polished Mahogany/Walnut (round leg)	16,790.
G-160	5' 3"	Satin Finishes (round leg)	16,790.
G-160	5' 3"	Queen Anne Polished Ebony	16,190.
G-160	5' 3"	Queen Anne Polished Mahogany/Walnut	16,790.
G-160	5' 3"	Queen Anne Satin Finishes	16,790.
G-160	5' 3"	with Renner hammers, add'l	550.
E-187	6' 1"	Polished Ebony	25,390.
E-187	6' 1"	Polished Mahogany/Walnut	26,990.
G-187	6' 1"	Polished Ebony	17,990.
G-187	6' 1"	Polished Mahogany/Walnut/Oak	18,990.
G-187	6' 1"	Polished White	18,990.
G-187	6' 1"	Satin Finishes	18,990.
G-187	6' 1"	Polished Ebony (round leg)	18,450.
G-187	6' 1"	Polished Mahogany/Walnut (round leg)	19,390.
G-187	6' 1"	Satin Finishes (round leg)	19,390.
G-187	6' 1"	Queen Anne Polished Ebony	18,450.
G-187	6' 1"	Queen Anne Polished Mahogany/Walnut	19,390.
G-187	6' 1"	Queen Anne Satin Finishes	19,390.
G-187	6' 1"	with Renner hammers, add'l	550.

Petrof

Note: Prices below do not include bench. Add from $220 to $630 (most are under $400), depending on choice of bench.

Verticals

115-I	46"	Pol. Walnut/Mahogany w/Designer Panel	7,700.
115-IC	46"	Chippendale Polished Walnut/Mahogany	7,700.
115-II	45"	Polished Ebony	6,700.
115-II D	45"	Polished Ebony/Walnut/Mahogany	7,500.
115-V	46"	Polished Ebony/Walnut/Mahogany	7,300.
115-VI	46"	Polished Ebony/Walnut/Mahogany	6,900.
115-VI	46"	Polished Walnut with Marquetry	7,300.
115-VI	46"	Pol. Walnut/Mahogany w/Designer Panel	7,300.
115-VI	46"	"Elegance" Polished Ebony w/Brass Trim	7,100.
125-III	50"	Polished Walnut/Mahogany	8,580.

*For explanation of terms and prices, please see pages 59–65.

Petrof (continued)

Model	Size	Style and Finish	Price*
125-III	50"	Polished Walnut/Mahogany with Fan Panels	8,780.
125-IV	50"	Polished Ebony	8,700.
126	50"	"Eleganté" Pol. Eby. w/Walnut&Brass Trim	9,180.
131	52"	Polished Ebony/Walnut/Mahogany	11,700.
135	53"	"Klasik" Polished Ebony	16,100.

Grands

Model	Size	Style and Finish	Price*
V	5' 3"	Polished Ebony/Walnut/Mahogany	22,200.
V DC	5' 3"	Demi-Chip. Pol. Ebony/Walnut/Mahogany	25,000.
IV	5' 8"	Polished Ebony/Walnut/Mahogany	23,800.
IV C	5' 8"	Chippendale Pol. Ebony/Walnut/Mahogany	29,400.
IV DC	5' 8"	Demi-Chip. Pol. Ebony/Walnut/Mahogany	25,800.
IV	5' 8"	"Klasik" Polished Ebony/Walnut/Mahogany	28,600.
III	6' 4"	Polished Ebony/Walnut/Mahogany	28,800.
III	6' 4"	"Majestic" Pol. Ebony/Walnut/Mahogany	30,800.
II	7' 9"	Polished Ebony/Walnut	43,000.
I	9' 3"	"Mistral" Polished Ebony	69,000.

PianoDisc

Prices for PianoDisc and QuietTime systems vary by piano manufacturer and installer. The following are suggested retail prices from PianoDisc. The usual dealer discounts may apply, especially as an incentive to purchase a piano.

Opus7 "Opulence," factory-installed or retrofitted	18,357.
Opus7 "Luxury," factory-installed or retrofitted	14,276.
Opus7 Performance Package option	2,733.
228 CFX System, factory-installed or retrofitted:	
Playback only	6,635.
Add for SymphonyPro Sound Module	1,115.
Add for TFT MIDI Record system	1,627.
Add for amplified speakers, pair	735.
Add for MX (Music Expansion) Basic	1,171.
Add for MX (Music Expansion) Platinum	1,758.
Add for PianoMute Rail	664.
PianoCD System	5,995.
QuietTime GT System (TFT MIDI Strip, MIDI interface board, pedal switches, cable, headphones, power supply, PianoMute rail)	2,409.

Model	Size	Style and Finish	Price*
MIDI Controller (TFT MIDI Strip, MIDI interface board,			
		pedal switches, cable, power supply)	2,031.
AudioForte			2,447.

Pleyel

Verticals

Model	Size	Style and Finish	Price*
Esprit	45"	Continental Polished Ebony	10,700.
Academie	45"	Polished Ebony	11,300.
Academie	45"	*Walnut*	11,700.
Academie	45"	*Polished White*	11,700.
P 118	47"	Polished Ebony	12,900.
P 118	47"	Polished Mahogany	14,600.
P 118	47"	*Walnut*	13,900.
P 118	47"	Cherry with Marquetry	14,100.
P 118	47"	Walnut with Leather	18,900.
P 118	47"	"Romantica Noyer" Walnut	13,900.
P 124	49"	Polished Ebony	14,200.
P 124	49"	*Walnut with Marquetry*	15,700.
P 124	49"	Cherry with Marquetry	15,700.
P 131	51"	Polished Ebony	18,900.
P 131	51"	Polished Mahogany	20,200.
P 131	51"	*With Sostenuto, add*	900.

Grands

Model	Size	Style and Finish	Price*
P 170	5' 7"	Polished Ebony	49,900.
P 170	5' 7"	Polished Mahogany	60,500.
P 170	5' 7"	Walnut	55,600.
P 190	6' 3"	Polished Ebony	59,300.
P 190	6' 3"	Cherry with Marquetry	69,900.
P 190	6' 3"	Polished Mahogany with Marquetry	69,900.
P 190	6' 3"	Poplar Burl	80,200.
P 190	6' 3"	Gilded Louis XVI	165,000.
P 190	6' 3"	Painted Decorations & Gilded Ornaments	111,000.
P 190	6' 3"	Painted Decorations w/o Gilded Ornaments	108,000.
P 280	9' 2"	Polished Ebony	169,000.

*For explanation of terms and prices, please see pages 59–65.

QRS / Pianomation

Prices for Pianomation systems vary by piano manufacturer, installer, and accessories. The following are approximate retail prices for installed systems from QRS. The usual dealer discounts may apply, especially as an incentive to purchase a piano.

Pianomation:	2000C Player System	5,320.
	2000CD+ Player System, CD player, speaker	6,300.
	Petine Player System, DVD ROM player, speaker	6,300.
	Petine Lite Player System	5,500.
	Other systems not yet priced.	
Playola:	With 2000C Player System	6,000.
	With 2000CD+ Player System	6,750.

Practice Session with record strip, piano-only sound, stop rail   950.

Remington

Also available in polished ivory, white, walnut, and cherry at same price as mahogany.

Verticals

Model	Size	Style and Finish	Price
RVM-108	43"	Continental Polished Ebony	2,790.
RVM-108	43"	Continental Polished Mahogany	2,990.
RV-43F	43"	Fr. Provincial Cherry/Mahogany/Walnut	3,190.
RV-43T	43"	Cherry	2,990.
RV-43T	43"	Mahogany/Walnut	3,190.
RVM-118	46-1/2"	Polished Ebony	3,190.
RVM-118	46-1/2"	Mahogany	3,390.
RVM-121	48"	Polished Ebony	3,390.
RVM-121	48"	Polished Mahogany	3,590.
RVM-131	52"	Polished Ebony	3,990.
RVM-131	52"	Polished Mahogany	4,190.

Grands

Model	Size	Style and Finish	Price
RG-150	5'	Polished Ebony	6,990.
RG-150	5'	Polished Mahogany	7,390.
RG-157	5' 2"	Polished Ebony	7,990.
RG-157	5' 2"	Polished Mahogany	8,390.
RG-175	5' 9"	Polished Ebony	9,190.
RG-175	5' 9"	Polished Mahogany	9,590.
RG-185	6' 1"	Polished Ebony	10,990.
RG-185	6' 1"	Polished Mahogany	11,390.

Ritmüller

Verticals

Model	Size	Style and Finish	Price*
UP-110R2	43-1/2"	Polished Ebony	3,570.
UP-110R2	43-1/2"	Polished Dark Mahogany/Walnut	3,610.
UP-118R4	43-1/2"	French Provincial Cherry	3,660.
UP-118R5	43-1/2"	Walnut	3,660.
UP-118R6	43-1/2"	American Country Oak	3,660.
UP-118R2	46-1/2"	"Scandinavian Design" Polished Ebony	4,060.
UP-118R2	46-1/2"	"Scandinavian Design" Pol. Dark Mahog.	4,130.
UP-118R3	46-1/2"	Cherry	5,030.
UP-120R	48"	Polished Ebony	4,650.
UP-120R	48"	Polished Dark Mahogany/Walnut	4,730.
UP-120R	48"	Polished White	4,730.
UP-120R1	48"	"European Design" Pol. Ebony w/Mahog.	4,770.
UP-120R2	48"	Chippendale Walnut/Mahogany	5,080.
UP-120R3	48"	"Euro-Modern" Polished Ebony	5,220.
UP-120R4	48"	French Provincial Cherry	5,080.
UP-120R6	48"	Queen Anne Cherry	5,380.
UP-120R7	48"	Italian Provincial Walnut	5,380.
UP-120R8	48"	American Classic Walnut	5,380.
UP-123R	48"	"Classic Euro" Polished Ebony	5,770.
UP-123R	48"	"Classic Euro" Polished Mahogany/Walnut	5,830.
UP-123R1	48"	"Deluxe European" Polished Ebony	5,780.
UP-125R	49"	"European" Polished Ebony w/Mahogany	6,220.
UP-125R2	49"	"Deluxe European" Pol. Ebony w/Mahog.	6,420.
UP-126R	49"	Polished Ebony	6,260.
UP-130R	51"	Polished Ebony (movable front)	6,400.
UP-130R	51"	Walnut (movable front)	6,450.
UP-130R	51"	Polished Dark Mahogany (movable front)	6,450.
UP-130R1	51"	Polished Ebony	6,340.
UP-130R2	51"	Polished Ebony	6,740.

Grands

Model	Size	Style and Finish	Price*
GP-148R	4' 10"	Ebony (round leg, brass trim)	9,390.
GP-148R	4' 10"	Polished Ebony (round leg, brass trim)	9,190.
GP-148R	4' 10"	Polished Mahogany (round leg, brass trim)	9,580.
GP-148R1	4' 10"	Polished Ebony (tapered leg, brass trim)	9,070.
GP-159R	5' 3"	Ebony (round leg, brass trim)	12,860.
GP-159R	5' 3"	Polished Ebony (round leg, brass trim)	12,520.
GP-159R	5' 3"	Mahogany (round leg, brass trim)	13,060.

*For explanation of terms and prices, please see pages 59–65.

Model	Size	Style and Finish	Price*

Ritmüller (continued)

Model	Size	Style and Finish	Price*
GP-159R	5' 3"	Pol. Mahog./Walnut (round leg, brass trim)	12,860.
GP-159R1	5' 3"	Ebony (tapered leg, brass trim)	12,900.
GP-159R1	5' 3"	Polished Ebony (tapered leg, brass trim)	12,540.
GP-159R1	5' 3"	Pol. Dark Mahog. (tapered leg, brass trim)	12,900.
GP-159R2	5' 3"	Louis XV Cherry	13,110.
GP-183R	6'	Ebony (round leg, brass trim)	16,580.
GP-183R	6'	Polished Ebony (round leg, brass trim)	16,120.
GP-183R1	6'	Ebony (tapered leg, brass trim)	16,190.
GP-183R1	6'	Polished Ebony (tapered leg, brass trim)	15,990.
GP-213R1	7'	Polished Ebony	22,600.
GP-275R1	9'	Polished Ebony	73,800.

Samick

Verticals

Model	Size	Style and Finish	Price*
JS-042	42"	Continental Polished Ebony	2,750.
JS-042	42"	Continental Polished Mahogany/Walnut	2,850.
JS-042	42"	Continental Cherry/Walnut	2,850.
JS-042	42"	Continental Polished Ivory	2,850.
JS-143F	43"	French Provincial Cherry	3,590.
JS-143M	43"	Mediterranean Brown Oak	3,590.
JS-143T	43"	Mahogany	3,590.
JS-115	45"	Ebony and Polished Ebony	3,190.
JS-115	45"	Satin and Polished Wood Finishes	3,190.
JS-247	46-1/2"	Ebony and Polished Ebony	4,700.
JS-247	46-1/2"	Satin and Polished Wood Finishes	4,700.
JS-121F	48"	French Provincial Polished Ebony	4,190.
JS-121F	48"	French Provincial Polished Mahogany	4,390.
JS-121M	48"	Mediterranean Polished Ebony	3,990.
JS-121M	48"	Mediterranean Polished Mahogany	4,270.
JS-131	52"	Polished Ebony	3,990.

Grands

Model	Size	Style and Finish	Price*
SIG-50	4' 11-1/2"	Ebony	8,590.
SIG-50	4' 11-1/2"	Polished Ebony	8,390.
SIG-50	4' 11-1/2"	Polished Mahogany	8,990.
SIG-50	4' 11-1/2"	French Provincial Polished Cherry	10,390.
SIG-54	5' 3"	Ebony	9,790.
SIG-54	5' 3"	Polished Ebony	9,590.

Model	Size	Style and Finish	Price*
SIG-54	5' 3"	Polished Mahogany	10,190.
SIG-57	5' 7"	Ebony	10,590.
SIG-57	5' 7"	Polished Ebony	10,390.
SIG-57	5' 7"	Polished Mahogany	10,990.
SIG-57L	5' 7"	Empire Polished Ebony	11,190.
SIG-57L	5' 7"	Empire Polished Mahogany	11,790.
SIG-61	6' 1"	Ebony	11,390.
SIG-61	6' 1"	Polished Ebony	11,190.
SIG-61	6' 1"	Polished Mahogany	11,790.

Sauter

Verticals

122	48"	"Ragazza" Polished Ebony	21,850.
122	48"	"Ragazza" Cherry	21,650.
122	48"	"Ragazza" Polished Cherry/Yew	25,300.
122	48"	"Vista" Polished Ebony	23,850.
122	48"	"Vista" Maple	22,780.
122	48"	"Vista" Cherry	23,700.
122	48"	School Piano Ebony/Beech Bright	18,990.
122	48"	"M-Line M2" Polished Ebony	28,200.
122	48"	Peter Maly "Pure Noble" Polished Ebony	29,970.
128	51"	"M-Line M1" Polished Ebony	31,700.
128	51'"	"Competence" Polished Ebony	26,990.
128	51"	"Competence" Walnut	25,700.

Grands

185	6' 1"	"Delta" Polished Ebony	61,140.
185	6' 1"	"Delta" Polished Pyramid Mahogany	67,500.
185	6' 1"	"Delta" Polished Bubinga	67,500.
185	6' 1"	"Delta" Polished Rio Palisander	67,500.
185	6' 1"	"Delta" satin standard wood veneer	56,190.
206	6' 9"	Peter Maly "Vivace" Polished Ebony	86,350.
220	7' 3"	"Omega" Polished Ebony	77,160.
220	7' 3"	"Omega" Polished Pyramid Mahogany	84,500.
220	7' 3"	"Omega" satin standard wood veneer	73,060.
275	9'	"Concert" Polished Ebony	129,220.

*For explanation of terms and prices, please see pages 59–65.

Schell, Lothar

Verticals

Model	Size	Style and Finish	Price*
LSU-110	43"	Polished Ebony	3,390.
LSU-110	43"	Polished Mahogany	3,590.
LSU-115F	45"	French Provincial Polished Ebony	3,590.
LSU-115F	45"	French Provincial Polished Mahogany	3,790.
LSU-45	45"	Mahogany and Polished Mahogany	3,790.
LSU-120	48"	Polished Ebony	3,900.
LSU-120	48"	Polished Mahogany	4,050.
LSU-122	48"	Polished Ebony	4,190.
LSU-122	48"	Polished Mahogany	4,340.

Grands

Model	Size	Style and Finish	Price*
LG-152	5'	Polished Ebony	8,790.
LG-152	5'	Polished Mahogany	9,190.
LG-152F	5'	French Provincial Polished Ebony	9,390.
LG-152F	5'	French Provincial Polished Mahogany	9,690.
LG-152R	5'	Polished Ebony (round legs)	9,390.
LG-152R	5'	Polished Mahogany (round legs)	9,790.
LG-165	5' 5"	Polished Ebony	9,590.
LG-165	5' 5"	Polished Mahogany	9,990.
LG-165F	5' 5"	French Provincial Polished Ebony	10,190.
LG-165F	5' 5"	French Provincial Polished Mahogany	10,590.
LG-165R	5' 5"	Polished Ebony (round legs)	10,190.
LG-165R	5' 5"	Polished Mahogany (round legs)	10,590.
LG-185	6' 1"	Polished Ebony	11,590.
LG-185	6' 1"	Polished Mahogany	11,990.
LG-185F	6' 1"	French Provincial Polished Ebony	12,190.
LG-185F	6' 1"	French Provincial Polished Mahogany	12,590.
LG-185R	6' 1"	Polished Ebony (round legs)	12,190.
LG-185R	6' 1"	Polished Mahogany (round legs)	12,590.
LG-215	7' 1"	Polished Ebony	18,290.

Schimmel

When not mentioned, satin finish available on special order at same price as high-polish finish.

Verticals

Model	Size	Style and Finish	Price*
112 S	44"	Open-Pore Ebony/Oak/Walnut	14,180.
116 ST	46"	Polished Ebony	12,980.

Model	Size	Style and Finish	Price*
116 ST	46"	Open-Pore Alder/Walnut	13,980.
116 ST	46"	Polished Mahogany/White	14,180.
P 120 E	48"	"Exquisit" Polished Ebony	15,380.
P 120 E	48"	"Exquisit" Open-Pore Alder	15,380.
P 120 E	48"	"Exquisit" Cherry	15,380.
P 120 E	48"	"Exquisit" Polished Mahogany	15,980.
P 120 E	48"	"Exquisit" Polished Ebony "Edition"	16,580.
P 120 I	48"	"International" Polished Ebony	14,980.
P 120 I	48"	"International" Polished Mahogany	15,580.
P 120 I	48"	"International" Polished White	15,580.
120 J	48"	"Centennial" Pol. Mahog. with Myrtle Inlay	17,380.
120 J	48"	"Centennial" Pol. Cherry with Yew Inlay	17,780.
120 RI	48"	"Royale Intarsia" Polished Mahogany	16,980.
120 RI	48"	"Royale Intarsia" Cherry	16,980.
120 S	48"	"School" Open-Pore Ebony/Oak	14,780.
P 120 T	48"	Polished Ebony	15,180.
P 120 T	48"	Open-Pore Alder/Beech/Walnut	15,180.
P 120 T	48"	Cherry	15,180.
P 120 T	48"	Polished White	15,780.
122 KE	49"	"Classic Exquisit" Polished Ebony	15,980.
122 KE	49"	"Classic Exquisit" O.P. Waxed Alder	15,980.
122 KE	49"	"Classic Exquisit" Cherry	15,980.
F 122 AC	49"	"Art Cubus" Polished Ebony	19,980.
F 122 AC	49"	"Art Cubus" Waxed Swiss Pear	19,980.
F 122 SE	49"	"Salon Exquisit" Polished Ebony	17,580.
M 124 R	49"	"Royale" Polished Ebony	16,780.
M 124 R	49"	"Royale" Polished Mahogany	18,780.
M 124 T	49"	Polished Ebony	15,980.
M 124 T	49"	Polished Ebony w/Oval Decoration	16,580.
M 124 T	49"	Polished Mahogany	17,580.
M 124 T	49"	Polished Mahogany w/Oval Decoration	17,980.
M 124 T	49"	Open-Pore Walnut Antique	17,180.
S 125 DN	49"	"Diamond Noblesse" Polished Ebony	21,180.
S 125 DN	49"	"Diamond Noblesse" Polished Mahogany	21,980.
S 125 DP	49"	"Diamond Prestige" Polished Ebony	21,180.
S 125 DP	49"	"Diamond Prestige" Polished Mahogany	21,980.
130 T	51"	Polished Ebony	17,580.
130 T	51"	Polished Ebony w/Oval Decoration	17,780.
130 T	51"	Polished Mahogany/Walnut	19,180.
130 T	51"	Open-Pore Walnut	18,580.
O 132 DT	52"	"Diamond Tradition" Polished Ebony	21,980.

*For explanation of terms and prices, please see pages 59–65.

123

Model	Size	Style and Finish	Price*

Schimmel (continued)

Model	Size	Style and Finish	Price*
O 132 DT	52"	"Diamond Tradition" Pol. Mahogany	23,980.
O 132 EM	52"	"Edition Manufactum" Mahogany/Walnut	34,980.

Grands

Model	Size	Style and Finish	Price*
GP 169 DE	5' 7"	"Diamond Edition" Polished Ebony	42,180.
GP 169 DE	5' 7"	"Diamond Edition" Pol. Flame Mahogany	45,780.
GP 169 DE	5' 7"	"Diamond Edition" Polished Bubinga	45,780.
GP 169 DE	5' 7"	"Diamond Edition" Pol. Bird's-Eye Maple	45,780.
GP 169 DE	5' 7"	"Diamond Edition" Macassar	45,780.
GP 169 DE	5' 7"	"Diamond Edition" Polished White	45,780.
GP 169 DE	5' 7"	"Diamond Edition" "Red Diamond"	45,780.
GP 169 E	5' 7"	"Empire" Mahogany and Pol. Mahogany	50,180.
GP 169 T	5' 7"	Polished Ebony	39,180.
GP 169 T	5' 7"	Polished Mahogany/White	40,380.
GP 169 T	5' 7"	"Hidden Beauty" Pol. Ebony w/Bubinga	41,980.
GP 169 TE	5' 7"	"Exquisit" Polished Ebony	41,980.
GP 169 TE	5' 7"	"Exquisit" Polished Mahogany/White	43,180.
GP 169 TE-I	5' 7"	"Exquisit" Polished Mahogany Intarsia	43,780.
GP 169 TJ	5' 7"	"Centennial" Polished Ebony	41,580.
GP 169 TJ	5' 7"	"Centennial" Polished Mahogany/White	42,780.
SP 189 DE	6' 3"	"Diamond Edition" Polished Ebony	45,380.
SP 189 DE	6' 3"	"Diamond Edition" Pol. Flame Mahogany	48,980.
SP 189 DE	6' 3"	"Diamond Edition" Polished Bubinga	48,980.
SP 189 DE	6' 3"	"Diamond Edition" Pol. Bird's-Eye Maple	48,980.
SP 189 DE	6' 3"	"Diamond Edition" Macassar	48,980.
SP 189 DE	6' 3"	"Diamond Edition" Polished White	48,980.
SP 189 DE	6' 3"	"Diamond Edition" "Red Diamond"	48,980.
SP 189 E	6' 3"	"Empire" Mahogany and Pol. Mahogany	53,180.
SP 189 NWS	6' 3"	"Nikolaus W. Schimmel Special Edition"	53,780.
SP 189 T	6' 3"	Polished Ebony	42,380.
SP 189 T	6' 3"	Polished Walnut/Mahogany/White	43,580.
SP 189 T	6' 3"	"Hidden Beauty" Pol. Ebony w/Bubinga	45,380.
SP 189 TE	6' 3"	"Exquisit" Polished Ebony	45,180.
SP 189 TE	6' 3"	"Exquisit" Polished Mahogany/White	46,380.
SP 189 TE-I	6' 3"	"Exquisit" Polished Mahogany Intarsia	46,980.
SP 189 TJ	6' 3"	"Centennial" Polished Ebony	44,780.
SP 189 TJ	6' 3"	"Centennial" Polished Mahogany	45,980.
CC 213 ART	7'	"Art Edition" Pol. Ebony w/color motifs	141,000.
CC 213 DE	7'	"Diamond Edition" Polished Ebony	48,580.
CC 213 DE	7'	"Diamond Edition" Pol. Flame Mahogany	52,180.

Model	Size	Style and Finish	Price*
CC 213 DE	7'	"Diamond Edition" Polished Bubinga	52,180.
CC 213 DE	7'	"Diamond Edition" Pol. Bird's-Eye Maple	52,180.
CC 213 DE	7'	"Diamond Edition" Macassar	52,180.
CC 213 DE	7'	"Diamond Edition" Polished White	52,180.
CC 213 DE	7'	"Diamond Edition" "Red Diamond"	52,180.
CC 213 G	7'	*"Transparent" Clear Acrylic and White*	119,000.
CC 213 NWS	7'	"Nikolaus W. Schimmel Special Edition"	57,980.
CC 213 T	7'	Polished Ebony	45,580.
CC 213 T	7'	Polished Mahogany/Walnut/White	46,780.
CC 213 T	7'	"Hidden Beauty" Pol. Ebony w/Bubinga	48,580.
CC 213 TE	7'	"Exquisit" Polished Ebony	48,380.
CC 213 TE	7'	"Exquisit" Polished Mahogany/White	49,580.
CC 213 TJ	7'	"Centennial" Polished Ebony	47,980.
CC 213 TJ	7'	"Centennial" Polished Mahogany/White	49,180.
CO 256 T	8' 4"	Polished Ebony	73,000.

Schulze Pollmann

Verticals

114/P4	45"	Polished Ebony	7,190.
114/P4	45"	Polished Mahogany/Walnut	7,390.
114/P4	45"	Polished Peacock Ebony	7,790.
114/P4	45"	Polished Peacock Mahogany/Walnut	7,790.
118/P8	46"	Polished Ebony	11,190.
118/P8	46"	Polished Briar Walnut	11,990.
118/P8	46"	Polished Feather or Peacock Mahogany	11,990.
126/P6	50"	Polished Ebony	12,790.
126/P6	50"	Polished Peacock Ebony	13,390.
126/P6	50"	Polished Peacock Mahogany/Cherry/Walnut	13,390.
126/P6	50"	Peacock Walnut	13,390.
126/P6	50"	Polished Briar Mahogany/Walnut	13,390.

Grands

160/GK	5' 3"	Polished Ebony (spade leg)	26,390.
160/GK	5' 3"	Polished Ebony (round leg)	27,390.
160/GK	5' 3"	Polished Briar Mahogany (spade leg)	30,390.
160/GK	5' 3"	Polished Briar Mahogany (round leg)	32,390.
160/GK	5' 3"	Peacock Mahogany (spade leg)	34,390.
160/GKR	5' 3"	Polished Ebony (spade leg)	29,390.
160/GKR	5' 3"	Polished Ebony (round leg)	30,390.
160/GKR	5' 3"	Polished Briar Mahogany (spade leg)	32,390.

*For explanation of terms and prices, please see pages 59–65.

Model	Size	Style and Finish	Price*

Schulze Pollmann (continued)

Model	Size	Style and Finish	Price*
160/GKR	5' 3"	Polished Briar Mahogany (round leg)	34,390.
160/GKR	5' 3"	Polished Briar Mahogany (French leg)	36,390.
160/GKR	5' 3"	Peacock Mahogany (spade leg)	34,990.
160/GKR	5' 3"	Peacock Cherry (spade leg)	34,990.
190/F	6' 2"	Polished Ebony	39,390.
190/F	6' 2"	Polished Briar Mahogany	43,190.
190/F	6' 2"	Polished Briar Walnut	43,990.
190/F	6' 2"	Polished Feather Mahogany	46,390.
197/G2	6' 7"	Polished Ebony	44,390.
197/G2	6' 7"	Polished Briar Mahogany/Walnut	48,390.

Seidl & Sohn

Prices do not include bench.

Verticals

Model	Size	Style and Finish	Price
SL 109	43"	Continental Polished Ebony	6,971.
SL 109	43"	Cont. Oak/Walnut/Mahogany/Alder/Beech	6,744.
SL 109	43"	Continental Polished Walnut/Mahogany	7,069.
SL 109	43"	Continental Polished White	7,164.
SL 113	46"	Polished Ebony	7,164.
SL 113	46"	Oak/Walnut/Mahogany/Alder/Beech	6,904.
SL 113	46"	Polished Walnut/Mahogany	7,265.
SL 113	46"	Polished White	7,326.
SL 117	47"	Demi-Chippendale Walnut	7,809.
SL 120	48"	Polished Ebony	7,550.
SL 120	48"	Oak/Walnut/Mahogany/Alder/Beech	7,261.
SL 120	48"	Polished Walnut/Mahogany	7,662.
SL 120	48"	Polished White	7,712.
SL 127	51"	Polished Ebony	8,680.
SL 127	51"	Polished Walnut/Mahogany	8,815.
SL 127	51"	Polished White	8,894.
		Renner Action, add'l	918.

Seiler

Verticals

Model	Size	Style and Finish	Price
116	46"	"Primus" Polished Ebony	14,360.
116	46"	"Mondial" Open-Pore Ebony	16,160.
116	46"	"Mondial" Open-Pore Walnut/Mahog./Oak	16,160.

Model	Size	Style and Finish	Price*
116	46"	"Mondial" Polished Mahogany	16,900.
116	46"	"Mondial" Open-Pore Maple/Alder	16,320.
116	46"	"Mondial" Open-Pore Cherry	17,220.
116	46"	"Mondial" Open-Pore Swiss Pear	16,680.
116	46"	"Mondial" Open-Pore Apple Heartwood	17,220.
116	46"	"Mondial" Polished Burl Rosewood	18,700.
116	46"	"Jubilee" Polished Ebony	17,340.
116	46"	"Jubilee" Polished White	17,620.
116	46"	Chippendale Open-Pore Walnut	16,320.
116	46"	"Escorial" Open-Pore Cherry Intarsia	17,620.
122	48"	"School" Open-Pore Ebony/Walnut/Oak	16,060.
122	48"	"Primus" Polished Ebony	17,120.
122	48"	"Konsole" Open-Pore Ebony	16,820.
122	48"	"Konsole" Polished Ebony	17,940.
122	48"	"Konsole" Open-Pore Walnut/Maple/Oak	16,820.
122	48"	"Konsole" Polished Walnut Rootwood	24,300.
122	48"	"Konsole" Maple Burl	17,500.
122	48"	"Konsole" Open-Pore Cherry	17,640.
122	48"	"Konsole" Polished Burl Rosewood	20,760.
122	48"	"Konsole" Polished Brown Ash	20,760.
122	48"	"Konsole" Polished Mahogany	18,520.
122	48"	"Konsole" Polished Redwood/Myrtle Burl	21,820.
122	48"	"Konsole" Polished White	18,560.
122	48"	"Vienna" Polished Ebony w/Pilaster	18,440.
122	48"	"Vienna" Polished Ebony w/Pilaster & Oval	18,640.
122	48"	"Vienna" Pol. Mahogany w/ Flower Inlays	20,760.
122	48"	"Vienna" Polished Walnut w/ Flower Inlays	20,760.
122	48"	"Vienna" Maple with Pilaster	18,440.
122	48"	"Vienna" Maple with Pilaster & Oval	18,640.
132	52"	"Concert SMR" Polished Ebony	22,880.
132	52"	"Concert SMR" Polished Ebony w/Oval	23,560.
132	52"	"Concert SMR" Polished Ebony w/Candle	23,520.
132	52"	"Concert SMR" Polished Ebony w/Panels	23,680.
132	52"	"Concert SMR" Open-Pore Walnut	22,200.
132	52"	"Concert SMR" Polished Mahogany	23,580.
132	52"	"Concert SMR" Polished Burl Rosewood	25,160.
132	52"	"Concert SMR" Pol. Yew/Ash Rootwood	27,120.
132	52"	"Concert SMR" Polished Burl Maple	28,040.
132	52"	"Limited Edition" Polished Ebony	26,380.
132	52"	"Limited Ed." Pol. Ebony w/Oval or Pilaster	26,920.
132	52"	"Limited Ed." Pol. Ebony w/Oval & Pilaster	27,440.

*For explanation of terms and prices, please see pages 59–65.

Seiler (continued)

Grands

180	5' 11"	"Terrestre"	161,980.
180	5' 11"	"Suspension"	175,980.
186	6' 1"	"Maestro" Polished Ebony	50,480.
186	6' 1"	"Maestro" Open-Pore Walnut/Mahogany	50,580.
186	6' 1"	"Maestro" Polished Walnut/Mahogany	53,980.
186	6' 1"	"Maestro" Polished Pyramid Mahogany	70,840.
186	6' 1"	"Maestro" Polished Burl Rosewood	63,140.
186	6' 1"	"Maestro" Polished Flamed Maple	63,780.
186	6' 1"	"Maestro" Polished Peacock Maple	70,840.
186	6' 1"	"Maestro" Polished Laurel Rootwood	70,840.
186	6' 1"	"Maestro" Polished White	51,720.
186	6' 1"	Chippendale Open-Pore Walnut	53,840.
186	6' 1"	"Westminster" Polished Mahogany, Intarsia	70,840.
186	6' 1"	"Florenz" Polished Walnut/Myrtle, Intarsia	70,840.
186	6' 1"	"Florenz" Polished Mahog./Myrtle, Intarsia	70,840.
186	6' 1"	"Louvre" Polished Ebony	56,820.
186	6' 1"	"Louvre" Polished Cherry, Intarsia	70,840.
186	6' 1"	"Louvre" Polished White	57,780.
186	6' 1"	"Prado" Polished Brown Ash	72,860.
186	6' 1"	"Prado" Polished Burl Redwood	75,440.
186	6' 1"	"Stella" Polished Maple Rootwood, Intarsia	87,000.
186	6' 1"	"Showmaster" Chrome/Brass/Polyester	141,120.
208	6' 10"	Polished Ebony	56,960.
208	6' 10"	"Empire 1897" Open-Pore Blue w/Brass	179,820.
208	6' 10"	"Solitaire" Custom with Painting	202,680.
208	6' 10"	"Solitaire" Custom without Painting	164,580.
242	8'	Polished Ebony	78,940.
278	9' 1"	Polished Ebony	92,720.

Sohmer (Persis International)

Verticals

S-126	50"	Polished Ebony	7,790.
S-126	50"	Polished Mahogany	7,990.

Grands

S-160	5' 3"	Polished Ebony	17,790.
S-160	5' 3"	Polished Mahogany	18,390.

Model	Size	Style and Finish	Price*
S-180	5' 10"	Polished Ebony	19,790.
S-180	5' 10"	Polished Mahogany	20,390.
S-218	7' 2"	Polished Ebony	33,990.

Sohmer & Co. (SMC)

Verticals

34F	42"	French Provincial Semi-Gloss Cherry	5,590.
34R	42"	Renaissance Semi-Gloss Walnut/Cherry	5,590.
34T	42"	Semi-Gloss Mahogany/Walnut	5,590.
45F	45"	French Provincial Semi-Gloss Cherry	6,390.
45R	45"	Renaissance Semi-Gloss Walnut/Cherry	6,390.
45S	45"	Ebony/Walnut	5,990.
45T	45"	Semi-Gloss Mahogany/Walnut	6,390.

Grands

50F	5'	Fr. Provincial Semi-Gloss Mahog./Cherry	17,190.
50T	5'	Ebony	12,990.
50T	5'	Polished Ebony	11,990.
50T	5'	Semi-Gloss Mahogany/Walnut/Cherry	15,190.
63E	5' 4"	Empire Semi-Gloss Mahog./Walnut/Cherry	16,990.
63F	5' 4"	Fr. Prov. Semi-Gloss Mahog/Walnut/Cherry	17,790.
63H	5' 4"	Hepplewhite S-G Mahog./Walnut/Cherry	17,190.
63T	5' 4"	Ebony	14,590.
63T	5' 4"	Polished Ebony	12,990.
63T	5' 4"	Semi-Gloss Mahogany/Walnut/Cherry	15,790.
77E	5' 9"	Empire Semi-Gloss Mahog./Walnut/Cherry	17,390.
77F	5' 9"	Fr. Prov. Semi-Gloss Mahog/Walnut/Cherry	18,190.
77H	5' 9"	Hepplewhite S-G Mahog./Walnut/Cherry	17,190.
77T	5' 9"	Ebony	14,990.
77T	5' 9"	Polished Ebony	13,990.
77T	5' 9"	Semi-Gloss Mahogany/Walnut/Cherry	16,190.
90H	6' 2"	Hepplewhite S-G Mahog./Walnut/Cherry	17,390.
90T	6' 2"	Ebony	15,190.
90T	6' 2"	Polished Ebony	14,990.
90T	6' 2"	Semi-Gloss Mahogany	16,390.
95T	6' 8"	Ebony	21,200.
95T	6' 8"	Polished Ebony	21,000.
95T	6' 8"	Semi-Gloss Mahogany/Walnut/Cherry	22,200.

*For explanation of terms and prices, please see pages 59–65.

Steck, Geo.

Verticals

Model	Size	Style and Finish	Price
US 09	43"	Continental Polished Ebony	2,870.
US 09	43"	Continental Cherry/Mahogany/Walnut	2,930.
US 09	43"	Continental Pol. Beech/Mahogany/Walnut	2,990.
US 09	43"	Continental Polished Ivory/White	2,990.
US 09L	43"	Continental Polished Ebony	2,950.
US 09L	43"	Continental Polished Mahogany/Walnut	3,070.
US 09L	43"	Continental Polished White	3,070.
CS 12FD	44"	French Provincial Brown Oak/Cherry	3,490.
CS 12M	44"	Mediterranean Brown Oak/Cherry	3,490.
US 12F	44"	Cherry/Mahogany	3,260.
US 12T	44"	Polished Ebony	3,080.
US 12T	44"	Walnut/Cherry/Mahogany	3,140.
US 12T	44"	Polished Mahogany/Walnut/White	3,200.
CS 13M1D	44-1/2"	Brown Oak	3,790.
CS 16AT	45-1/2"	Brown Oak/Cherry	3,870.
CS 16ATD	45-1/2"	Cherry	3,990.
CS 16F	45-1/2"	French Provincial Cherry/Brown Oak	3,650.
CS 16FD	45-1/2"	French Provincial Cherry	3,770.
CS 16IP	45-1/2"	Italian Provincial Walnut/Cherry	3,670.
CS 16IPD	45-1/2"	Italian Provincial Cherry	3,790.
CS 16QA	45-1/2"	Queen Anne Cherry/Brown Oak	3,970.
CS 16QAD	45-1/2"	Queen Anne Cherry	4,090.
CS 16T	45-1/2"	Cherry/Brown Oak/Walnut	3,870.
US 16ST	45-1/2"	Brown Oak/Cherry (school)	3,200.
US 16STL	45-1/2"	Brown Oak/Cherry	3,500.
US 16TC	45-1/2"	Polished Ebony	3,240.
US 16TC	45-1/2"	Polished Mahogany/Walnut	3,360.
CS 19F	47"	French Provincial Brown Oak/Cherry	3,700.
CS 19FD	47"	French Provincial Brown Oak/Cherry	3,820.
CS 19MD	47"	Mediterranean Brown Oak/Cherry	3,820.
CS 19M1D	47"	Mediterranean Cherry	3,820.
CS 19QAD	47"	Cherry	4,190.
US 19F	47"	Demi-Chippendale Polished Ebony	3,320.
US 19F	47"	Demi-Chippendale Cherry/Mahogany	3,380.
US 19F	47"	Demi-Chip. Pol. Cherry/Mahog./Walnut	3,440.
US 19F	47"	Demi-Chippendale Polished Ivory/White	3,440.
US 19T	47"	Polished Ebony	3,200.
US 19T	47"	Cherry	3,260.

Model	Size	Style and Finish	Price*
US 19T	47"	Polished Mahogany/Brown Oak/Walnut	3,320.
US 22F	48"	Demi-Chippendale Polished Ebony	3,490.
US 22F	48"	Demi-Chippendale Pol. Mahogany/Walnut	3,610.
US 22T	48"	Ebony	3,430.
US 22T	48"	Polished Ebony	3,370.
US 22T	48"	Polished Mahogany/Walnut/White	3,490.
US 23FD	48-1/2"	Cherry/Mahogany	3,800.
US 23FD	48-1/2"	Polished Walnut/Mahogany	3,860.
US 23TD	48-1/2"	Polished Ebony	3,620.
US 23TD	48-1/2"	Polished Mahogany/Walnut	3,740.
US 32FD	52"	Polished Mahogany	3,980.
US 32T	52"	Ebony	3,680.
US 32T	52"	Polished Ebony	3,620.
US 32TD	52"	Polished Mahogany	3,860.
Grands			
GS 42	4' 8"	Polished Ivory/White	8,620.
GS 42	4' 8"	Polished Mahogany/Walnut	8,820.
GS 42D	4' 8"	Ebony	8,740.
GS 42D	4' 8"	Polished Ebony	8,540.
GS 42D	4' 8"	Cherry/Mahogany/Walnut	9,140.
GS 42D	4' 8"	Polished Cherry/Mahogany/Walnut	8,940.
GS 42D	4' 8"	Polished Bubinga	9,540.
GS 42F	4' 8"	French Provincial Pol. Mahogany/Walnut	9,420.
GS 42FD	4' 8"	French Provincial Polished Ebony	9,140.
GS 42FD	4' 8"	French Prov. Pol. Cherry/Mahog./Walnut	9,540.
GS 52	5'	Polished Mahogany/Walnut	9,660.
GS 52D	5'	Ebony	9,580.
GS 52D	5'	Polished Ebony	9,380.
GS 52D	5'	Mahogany	9,980.
GS 52D	5'	Polished Mahogany/Walnut	9,780.
GS 52D	5'	Polished White	9,580.
GS 52F	5'	French Provincial Polished Mahogany	10,380.
GS 52FD	5'	French Provincial Cherry/Mahogany	10,580.
GS 52FD	5'	French Prov. Pol. Cherry/Mahog./Walnut	10,380.
GS 52LD	5'	Louis XVI Polished Ebony	9,860.
GS 62	5' 4"	Polished Ebony	10,290.
GS 62	5' 4"	Polished Cherry/Mahogany/Walnut	10,490.
GS 62	5' 4"	Polished Bubinga	11,290.
GS 62	5' 4"	Polished White	10,490.
GS 62D	5' 4"	Ebony	10,610.

*For explanation of terms and prices, please see pages 59–65.

Model	Size	Style and Finish	Price*

Steck, Geo. (continued)

Model	Size	Style and Finish	Price*
GS 62D	5' 4"	Polished Ebony	10,410.
GS 62D	5' 4"	Polished Mahogany/Walnut	10,810.
GS 62D	5' 4"	Polished Bubinga	11,410.
GS 62D	5' 4"	Polished White	10,610.
GS 62F	5' 4"	French Provincial Polished Ebony	10,890.
GS 62F	5' 4"	French Provincial Polished Mahogany	11,290.
GS 62FD	5' 4"	French Provincial Polished Mahogany	11,410.
GS 62FD	5' 4"	French Provincial Polished White	11,210.
GS 62FD	5' 4"	French Provincial Cherry	11,610.
GS 72	5' 8"	Polished Ebony	11,320.
GS 72	5' 8"	Cherry	11,920.
GS 72	5' 8"	Pol. Beech/Brown Oak/Mahogany/Walnut	11,720.
GS 72D	5' 8"	Ebony	11,640.
GS 72D	5' 8"	Polished Ebony	11,440.
GS 72D	5' 8"	Cherry/Mahogany	12,040.
GS 72D	5' 8"	Pol. Cherry/Brown Oak/Mahogany/Walnut	11,840.
GS 72D	5' 8"	Polished Bubinga	12,440.
GS 72F	5' 8"	French Provincial Polished Ebony	11,920.
GS 72F	5' 8"	French Provincial Cherry	12,520.
GS 72F	5' 8"	French Provincial Polished Mahogany	12,320.
GS 72FD	5' 8"	French Provincial Cherry	12,640.
GS 72FD	5' 8"	French Provincial Polished Mahogany	12,440.
GS 72L	5' 8"	Louis XVI Polished Ebony	11,920.
GS 72L	5' 8"	Louis XVI Polished Mahogany	12,320.
GS 72LD	5' 8"	Louis XVI Polished Mahogany	12,320.
GS 87	6' 2"	Walnut	12,940.
GS 87	6' 2"	Polished Mahogany/Walnut	12,740.
GS 87D	6' 2"	Ebony	12,660.
GS 87D	6' 2"	Polished Ebony	12,460.
GS 87D	6' 2"	Mahogany	13,060.
GS 87D	6' 2"	Polished Mahogany/Walnut	12,860.
GS 87F	6' 2"	French Provincial Polished Mahogany	13,340.
GS 87FD	6' 2"	French Provincial Polished Mahogany	13,460.
GS 87L	6' 2"	Louis XVI Polished Ebony	12,820.
GS 87L	6' 2"	Louis XVI Polished Mahogany	13,220.
GS 87LD	6' 2"	Louis XVI Ebony	13,140.
GS 87LD	6' 2"	Louis XVI Polished Ebony	12,940.
GS 87LD	6' 2"	Louis XVI Mahogany	13,540.
GS 87LD	6' 2"	Louis XVI Polished Mahogany	13,340.

Model	Size	Style and Finish	Price*
GS 208D	6' 10"	Polished Ebony	15,600.
GS 228D	7' 6"	Polished Ebony	19,600.
GS 278D	9' 2"	Polished Ebony	47,600.

Steinberg, Gerh.

Verticals

Model	Size	Style and Finish	Price*
HM-109	43"	Continental Polished Ebony	4,490.
HM-109	43"	Continental Pol. Mahog./Walnut/Oak/White	4,790.
HM-109	43"	Continental Satin Finish	4,790.
HM-109	43"	Polished Ebony (straight leg)	4,790.
HM-109	43"	Polished Mahogany/Walnut/Oak/White	4,990.
HM-109	43"	Satin Finish	4,990.
HM-109	43"	Queen Anne Polished Ebony	4,990.
HM-109	43"	Queen Anne Polished Mahogany/Walnut	5,250.
HM-109	43"	Queen Anne Walnut	5,250.
HM-115	45"	Walnut/Mahogany/Oak (square leg)	5,490.
HM-115	45"	Contemporary Walnut/Mahogany/Oak	5,490.
HM-115	45"	Queen Anne Walnut/Mahogany/Oak	5,490.
HM-115	45"	Country French Mahogany/Oak	5,490.
HM-116	46"	Deco Leg Polished Ebony	4,990.
HM-116	46"	Deco Leg Polished Ebony w/Walnut Trim	5,190.
HM-116	46"	Deco Leg Polished Mahogany/Oak/White	5,390.
HM-116	46"	Queen Anne Polished Ebony	5,190.
HM-116	46"	Queen Anne Polished Mahogany/Walnut	5,490.
EV-123	48"	Polished Ebony	6,190.
EV-123	48"	Polished Ebony w/Pommele Center	6,290.
EV-123	48"	Polished Mahogany/Walnut/Oak/White	6,390.
EV-123	48"	Satin Finish	6,390.
EV-123	48"	Queen Anne Polished Ebony	6,390.
EV-123	48"	Queen Anne Polished Mahogany/Walnut	6,590.
EV-125	49"	Polished Ebony	6,690.
EV-125	49"	Polished Ebony w/Pommele Center	6,790.
EV-125	49"	Polished Mahogany/Walnut/White	6,995.
EV-125	49"	Queen Anne Polished Ebony	6,890.
EV-125	49"	Queen Anne Polished Mahogany/Walnut	7,190.

*For explanation of terms and prices, please see pages 59–65.

Steinberg, Gerh. (continued)

Grands

Model	Size	Style and Finish	Price*
S-159	5' 3"	Polished Ebony	15,590.
S-159	5' 3"	Polished Mahogany/Walnut/Oak/White	16,190.
S-159	5' 3"	Satin Finish	16,190.
S-159	5' 3"	Polished Ebony (round leg)	15,890.
S-159	5' 3"	Polished Mahogany/Walnut (round leg)	16,490.
S-159	5' 3"	Satin Finish (round leg)	16,490.
S-159	5' 3"	Queen Anne Polished Ebony	15,890.
S-159	5' 3"	Queen Anne Polished Mahogany/Walnut	16,490.
S-159	5' 3"	Queen Anne Satin Finish	16,490.
S-186	6' 1"	Polished Ebony	17,690.
S-186	6' 1"	Polished Mahogany/Walnut/Oak/White	18,690.
S-186	6' 1"	Satin Finish	18,690.
S-186	6' 1"	Polished Ebony (round leg)	18,150.
S-186	6' 1"	Polished Mahogany/Walnut (round leg)	18,990.
S-186	6' 1"	Satin Finish (round leg)	18,990.
S-186	6' 1"	Queen Anne Polished Ebony	18,150.
S-186	6' 1"	Queen Anne Polished Mahogany/Walnut	18,990.
S-186	6' 1"	Queen Anne Satin Finish	18,990.

Steinberg, Wilh.

Verticals

Model	Size	Style and Finish	Price*
IQ 22	49"	Polished Ebony	14,422.
IQ 22	49"	Beech/Oak/Alder	14,422.
IQ 22	49"	Walnut/Mahogany	14,695.
IQ 22	49"	Cherry	15,322.
IQ 22	49"	Cherry with Yew	16,223.
IQ 22	49"	"Amadeus" Polished Ebony	15,909.
IQ 22	49"	"Amadeus" Mahogany/Walnut	16,223.
IQ 28	52"	Polished Ebony	18,011.
IQ 28	52"	Mahogany/Walnut	18,148.
IQ 28	52"	Cherry	18,435.
IQ 28	52"	Cherry with Yew	18,885.
IQ 28	52"	"Amadeus" Polished Ebony	18,885.
IQ 28	52"	"Amadeus" Cherry	19,308.
IQ 28	52"	"Passione" Polished Ebony	20,455.
IQ 28	52"	"Passione" Mahogany/Walnut	20,974.

Model	Size	Style and Finish	Price*
Grands			
IQ 77	5' 9"	Polished Ebony	45,906.
IQ 77	5' 9"	Mahogany/Walnut	47,271.
IQ 77	5' 9"	Cherry	48,158.
IQ 99	6' 3"	Polished Ebony	53,072.
IQ 99	6' 3"	Mahogany/Walnut	59,228.
IQ 99	6' 3"	Cherry	60,648.

Steingraeber & Söhne

This list includes only those models most likely to be offered to U.S. customers. Other models, styles, and finishes are available.

Verticals			
130	51"	Polished Ebony	36,853.
130	51"	Special Veneers	38,975.
138	54"	Polished Ebony	40,736.
138	54"	Polished Ebony with Wood Accents	42,736.
138	54"	"Baroque" Burl Walnut	53,478.
Grands			
168N	5' 6"	Polished Ebony	67,928.
168N	5' 6"	Special Veneers	79,454.
168K	5' 6"	"Classicism" Polished Ebony	79,104.
168K	5' 6"	"Classicism" Pol. Ebony w/Pyr. Mahogany	84,357.
168K	5' 6"	"Classicism" Pol. Ebony w/Burl Walnut	84,357.
205N	6' 9"	Polished Ebony	90,434.
205N	6' 9"	Special Veneers	102,794.
205K	6' 9"	"Classicism" Polished Ebony	101,187.
205K	6' 9"	"Classicism" Pol. Ebony w/Pyr. Mahogany	109,098.
205K	6' 9"	"Classicism" Pol. Ebony w/Burl Walnut	109,098.
E-272	8' 11"	Polished Ebony	179,014.

Steinway & Sons

Verticals			
4510	45"	Sheraton Ebony	20,600.
4510	45"	Sheraton Mahogany	22,700.
4510	45"	Sheraton Walnut	23,400.
4510	45"	Sheraton Dark Cherry	24,200.

*For explanation of terms and prices, please see pages 59–65.

Steinway & Sons (continued)

Model	Size	Style and Finish	Price*
4510	45"	Macassar Ebony	29,000.
4510	45"	Marbelized	28,200.
1098	46-1/2"	Ebony	19,600.
1098	46-1/2"	Mahogany	21,000.
1098	46-1/2"	Walnut	21,800.
1098	46-1/2"	Dark Cherry	22,600.
1098	46-1/2"	Marbelized	26,600.
K-52	52"	Ebony	25,600.
K-52	52"	Mahogany	28,800.
K-52	52"	Walnut	29,700.
K-52	52"	East Indian Rosewood	37,000.
K-52	52"	Marbelized	34,500.

Grands

Model	Size	Style and Finish	Price*
S	5' 1"	Ebony	42,100.
S	5' 1"	Mahogany	46,900.
S	5' 1"	Walnut	48,300.
S	5' 1"	Figured Sapele	51,000.
S	5' 1"	Dark Cherry	51,700.
S	5' 1"	Kewazinga Bubinga	52,400.
S	5' 1"	African Cherry	54,300.
S	5' 1"	Satinwood	57,500.
S	5' 1"	Anigre	57,500.
S	5' 1"	Santos Rosewood	58,400.
S	5' 1"	Pearwood	58,700.
S	5' 1"	East Indian Rosewood	59,500.
S	5' 1"	African Pommele	59,900.
S	5' 1"	Macassar Ebony	65,600.
S	5' 1"	Marbelized	58,400.
S	5' 1"	Hepplewhite Dark Cherry	52,600.
M	5' 7"	Ebony	45,500.
M	5' 7"	Mahogany	51,000.
M	5' 7"	Walnut	52,400.
M	5' 7"	Figured Sapele	54,500.
M	5' 7"	Dark Cherry	54,900.
M	5' 7"	Kewazinga Bubinga	57,200.
M	5' 7"	African Cherry	57,900.
M	5' 7"	Satinwood	61,100.
M	5' 7"	Anigre	61,100.
M	5' 7"	Santos Rosewood	62,900.

Model	Size	Style and Finish	Price*
M	5' 7"	Pearwood	63,300.
M	5' 7"	East Indian Rosewood	63,900.
M	5' 7"	African Pommele	64,300.
M	5' 7"	Macassar Ebony	70,300.
M	5' 7"	Marbelized	63,600.
M	5' 7"	Hepplewhite Dark Cherry	57,400.
M 1014A	5' 7"	Chippendale Mahogany	62,300.
M 1014A	5' 7"	Chippendale Walnut	63,700.
M 501A	5' 7"	Louis XV Walnut	81,700.
M 501A	5' 7"	Louis XV East Indian Rosewood	94,300.
L	5' 10-1/2"	Ebony	52,800.
L	5' 10-1/2"	Mahogany	57,000.
L	5' 10-1/2"	Walnut	58,400.
L	5' 10-1/2"	Figured Sapele	60,800.
L	5' 10-1/2"	Dark Cherry	61,800.
L	5' 10-1/2"	Kewazinga Bubinga	63,900.
L	5' 10-1/2"	African Cherry	65,300.
L	5' 10-1/2"	Satinwood	66,900.
L	5' 10-1/2"	Anigre	66,900.
L	5' 10-1/2"	Santos Rosewood	71,300.
L	5' 10-1/2"	Pearwood	71,700.
L	5' 10-1/2"	East Indian Rosewood	72,300.
L	5' 10-1/2"	African Pommele	72,600.
L	5' 10-1/2"	Macassar Ebony	79,000.
L	5' 10-1/2"	Marbelized	70,300.
L	5' 10-1/2"	Hepplewhite Dark Cherry	64,300.
L	5' 10-1/2"	Limited Edition 150th Historic Ebony	65,000.
L	5' 10-1/2"	Limited Ed. 150th Historic African Cherry	72,800.
L	5' 10-1/2"	Ltd. Ed. 150th Historic East Indian Rosewd.	83,000.
A	6' 2"	Ebony	57,600.
A	6' 2"	Limited Edition Tricentennial Pol. Ebony	75,700.
A	6' 2"	Limited Edition Lagerfield Ebony	85,000.
B	6' 10-1/2"	Ebony	64,300.
B	6' 10-1/2"	Mahogany	72,300.
B	6' 10-1/2"	Walnut	73,900.
B	6' 10-1/2"	Figured Sapele	77,300.
B	6' 10-1/2"	Dark Cherry	78,700.
B	6' 10-1/2"	Kewazinga Bubinga	80,900.
B	6' 10-1/2"	African Cherry	81,300.

*For explanation of terms and prices, please see pages 59–65.

Steinway & Sons (continued)

Model	Size	Style and Finish	Price*
B	6' 10-1/2"	Satinwood	81,700.
B	6' 10-1/2"	Anigre	81,700.
B	6' 10-1/2"	Santos Rosewood	89,900.
B	6' 10-1/2"	Pearwood	90,300.
B	6' 10-1/2"	East Indian Rosewood	91,100.
B	6' 10-1/2"	African Pommele	91,500.
B	6' 10-1/2"	Macassar Ebony	99,500.
B	6' 10-1/2"	Marbelized	85,600.
B	6' 10-1/2"	Hepplewhite Dark Cherry	81,700.
B	6' 10-1/2"	Limited Edition 150th Historic Ebony	86,200.
B	6' 10-1/2"	Limited Ed. 150th Historic African Cherry	96,600.
B	6' 10-1/2"	Ltd. Ed. 150th Historic East Indian Rosewd.	110,200.
D	8' 11-3/4"	Ebony	95,900.
D	8' 11-3/4"	Mahogany	105,000.
D	8' 11-3/4"	Walnut	106,700.
D	8' 11-3/4"	Figured Sapele	111,500.
D	8' 11-3/4"	Dark Cherry	117,600.
D	8' 11-3/4"	Kewazinga Bubinga	116,100.
D	8' 11-3/4"	African Cherry	118,900.
D	8' 11-3/4"	Satinwood	120,900.
D	8' 11-3/4"	Anigre	120,900.
D	8' 11-3/4"	Santos Rosewood	129,100.
D	8' 11-3/4"	Pearwood	129,500.
D	8' 11-3/4"	East Indian Rosewood	130,100.
D	8' 11-3/4"	African Pommele	130,500.
D	8' 11-3/4"	Macassar Ebony	142,500.
D	8' 11-3/4"	Hepplewhite Dark Cherry	118,100.
D	8' 11-3/4"	Limited Edition 150th Historic Ebony	119,000.
D	8' 11-3/4"	Limited Ed. 150th Historic African Cherry	131,000.
D	8' 11-3/4"	Ltd. Ed. 150th Historic East Indian Rosewd	151,800.

Grands (Hamburg)

I frequently get requests for prices of pianos made in Steinway's branch factory in Hamburg, Germany. Officially, these pianos are not sold in North America, but it is possible to order one through an American Steinway dealer, or to go to Europe and purchase one there. The following list shows approximately how much it would cost to purchase a Hamburg Steinway in Europe and have it shipped to the United States. The list was derived by taking the published retail price in Europe, subtracting the value-added tax not applicable to foreign purchasers, converting to U.S. dollars (the rate used here is 1 Euro = $1.30, but is obviously subject to change), and adding

Model	Size	Style and Finish	Price*

approximate charges for duty, air freight, crating, insurance, brokerage fees, and delivery. Only prices for grands in polished ebony are shown here. *Caution:* This list is published for general informational purposes only. The price that Steinway would charge for a piano ordered through an American Steinway dealer may be different. (Also, the cost of a trip to Europe to purchase the piano is not included!)

Model	Size	Style and Finish	Price
S-155	5' 1"	Polished Ebony	58,600.
M-170	5' 7"	Polished Ebony	64,000.
O-180	5' 10-1/2"	Polished Ebony	67,800.
A-188	6' 2"	Polished Ebony	72,300.
B-211	6' 11"	Polished Ebony	83,900.
C-227	7' 5-1/2"	Polished Ebony	98,200.
D-274	8' 11-3/4"	Polished Ebony	136,300.

Story & Clark

Verticals

Model	Size	Style and Finish	Price
111	45"	Continental Polished Ebony/Red Mahogany	2,790.
112	45"	"Arlington" Fruitwood/Cherry/Oak	3,990.
113	45"	"Charleston" Fruitwood/Cherry/Oak	3,990.
114	45"	Polished Ebony	3,790.
114	45"	Ebony/Oak/Fruitwood	3,790.
115	45"	Queen Anne Pol. Ebony/Red Mahogany	3,190.
115	45"	Queen Anne with QRS CD2000 Player	7,990.
115	45"	Queen Anne with QRS Wireless Player	8,990.
120	47"	Polished Ebony/Red and Brown Mahogany	4,390.
126	49"	Polished Ebony	3,990.
140	53"	Polished Red Mahogany	6,190.

Grands

Model	Size	Style and Finish	Price
152	5'	Ebony	8,490.
152	5'	Polished Ebony	7,890.
152	5'	Mahogany	8,490.
152	5'	Polished Red and Brown Mahogany	8,490.
152	5'	Polished Ebony w/ QRS CD2000 Player	11,990.
152	5'	Other Finishes w/QRS CD2000 Player	12,590.
152	5'	Polished Ebony w/QRS Wireless Player	12,990.
152	5'	Other Finishes w/QRS Wireless Player	13,590.
152 I	5'	"Imperial" Ebony and Polished Ebony	10,290.
152 I	5'	"Imperial" Polished Ebony w/CD2000	14,790.
152 I	5'	"Imperial" Polished Ebony w/Wireless	15,790.
152 S	5'	French Provincial Polished Ebony	9,890.

*For explanation of terms and prices, please see pages 59–65.

Model	Size	Style and Finish	Price*

Story & Clark (continued)

Model	Size	Style and Finish	Price*
152 S	5'	French Provincial Pol. Red/Brown Mahog.	9,890.
152 S	5'	French Provincial Mahogany	9,890.
152 S	5'	French Provincial All Finishes w/CD2000	14,390.
152 S	5'	French Provincial All Finishes w/Wireless	15,390.
165	5' 5"	Polished Ebony	9,490.
165	5' 5"	Polished Red and Brown Mahogany	10,090.
165	5' 5"	Polished Ebony w/CD2000 Player	13,990.
165	5' 5"	Other Finishes w/CD2000 Player	14,590.
165	5' 5"	Polished Ebony w/Wireless Player	14,990.
165	5' 5"	Other Finishes w/Wireless Player	15,590.
185	6' 1"	Polished Ebony	11,890.
185	6' 1"	Polished Ebony w/CD2000 Player	15,990.
185	6' 1"	Polished Ebony w/Wireless Player	16,990.
215	7'	Polished Ebony	16,990.
215	7'	Polished Ebony w/CD2000 Player	21,190.
215	7'	Polished Ebony w/Wireless Player	22,190.

Suzuki

Verticals

Model	Size	Style and Finish	Price*
AU-100	44-1/2"	Continental Polished Ebony	2,498.
AU-100	44-1/2"	Continental Polished Red Mahogany	2,498.
AU-200	46"	Polished Ebony	2,798.
AU-200	46"	Polished Red Mahogany	2,798.
AU-210	46"	French Provincial Polished Ebony	2,998.
AU-210	46"	French Provincial Polished Red Mahogany	2,998.
AU-300	48-1/2"	Polished Ebony	2,998.
AU-300	48-1/2"	Polished Red Mahogany	2,998.
AU-310	48-1/2"	"European Ornate" Polished Ebony	3,198.
AU-310	48-1/2"	"European Ornate" Polished Red Mahogany	3,198.

Grands

Model	Size	Style and Finish	Price*
AGP-500	5'	Polished Ebony	7,980.
AGP-500	5'	Polished Red and Brown Mahogany	8,380.
AGP-550	5' 5"	Polished Ebony	8,980.
AGP-550	5' 5"	Polished Red and Brown Mahogany	9,380.
AGP-600	6'	Polished Ebony	11,580.

Vogel

Verticals

Model	Size	Style and Finish	Price*
V-115 M	45"	Continental Polished Ebony	9,780.
V-115 M	45"	Continental Wood Finish	9,180.
V-115 T	45"	Polished Ebony	9,780.
V-115 T	45"	Polished White	10,580.

Grands

Model	Size	Style and Finish	Price*
V-160 CH	5' 4"	Chippendale Polished Ebony	25,380.
V-160 CH	5' 4"	Chippendale Polished Mahogany/Walnut	26,580.
V-160 CH	5' 4"	Chippendale Polished White	26,580.
V-160 R	5' 4"	"Royal" Polished Ebony	25,380.
V-160 R	5' 4"	"Royal" Polished Mahogany/Walnut	26,580.
V-160 R	5' 4"	"Royal" Polished White	26,580.
V-160 RI	5' 4"	"Royal" Polished Mahogany Intarsia	28,780.
V-160 RI	5' 4"	"Royal" Polished Flame Mahogany Coffer	28,780.
V-160 T	5' 4"	Polished Ebony	22,180.
V-160 T	5' 4"	Polished Mahogany/Walnut/White	23,380.
V-160 TI	5' 4"	Polished Mahogany Intarsia	30,580.
V-177 CH	5' 11"	Chippendale Polished Ebony	26,180.
V-177 CH	5' 11"	Chippendale Polished Mahogany/Walnut	27,380.
V-177 CH	5' 11"	Chippendale Polished White	27,380.
V-177 R	5' 11"	"Royal" Polished Ebony	26,180.
V-177 R	5' 11"	"Royal" Polished Mahogany/Walnut	27,380.
V-177 R	5' 11"	"Royal" Polished White	27,380.
V-177 RI	5' 11"	"Royal" Polished Mahogany Intarsia	29,580.
V-177 RI	5' 11"	"Royal" Polished Flame Mahogany Coffer	29,580.
V-177 T	5' 11"	Polished Ebony	22,980.
V-177 T	5' 11"	Polished Mahogany/Walnut/White	24,180.
V-177 TI	5' 11"	Polished Mahogany Intarsia	31,380.

Vose & Sons

Verticals

Model	Size	Style and Finish	Price*
113	45"	Polished Ebony	2,790.
113	45"	Polished Mahogany	2,890.

Grands

Model	Size	Style and Finish	Price*
147	4' 10"	Polished Ebony	7,190.
147	4' 10"	Polished Mahogany	7,590.

*For explanation of terms and prices, please see pages 59–65.

Walter, Charles R.

Verticals

Model	Size	Style and Finish	Price
1520	43"	Oak	8,660.
1520	43"	Cherry	8,950.
1520	43"	Walnut	8,970.
1520	43"	Mahogany	9,120.
1520	43"	Riviera Oak	8,640.
1520	43"	Italian Provincial Oak	8,670.
1520	43"	Italian Provincial Walnut	8,990.
1520	43"	Italian Provincial Mahogany	9,140.
1520	43"	French Provincial Oak	8,990.
1520	43"	Fr. Provincial Walnut/Mahogany/Cherry	9,240.
1520	43"	Country Classic Oak	8,720.
1520	43"	Country Classic Cherry	8,870.
1520	43"	Queen Anne Oak	9,050.
1520	43"	Queen Anne Cherry/Mahogany	9,240.
1500	45"	Ebony	8,420.
1500	45"	Semi-Gloss Ebony	8,530.
1500	45"	Polished Ebony	8,630.
1500	45"	Oak	8,000.
1500	45"	Walnut	8,460.
1500	45"	Mahogany	8,580.
1500	45"	Cherry/Gothic Oak	8,560.

Grands

Model	Size	Style and Finish	Price
W-190	6' 4"	Ebony	36,670.
W-190	6' 4"	Semi-Polished and Polished Ebony	37,610.
W-190	6' 4"	Mahogany/Walnut/Cherry	38,290.
W-190	6' 4"	Open-Pore Walnut	37,380.
W-190	6' 4"	Oak	35,260.
W-190	6' 4"	Semi-Polished and Polished Mahogany	39,260.
W-190	6' 4"	Semi-Polished and Polished Walnut	39,260.
W-190	6' 4"	Semi-Polished and Polished Cherry	39,260.
W-190	6' 4"	Chippendale Mahogany/Cherry	39,490.
W-190	6' 4"	Chippendale Semi-Pol. and Pol. Mahogany	40,420.
W-190	6' 4"	Chippendale Semi-Pol. and Polished Cherry	40,420.

Weber

"Legend" Verticals

Model	Size	Style and Finish	Price*
WLE 410	41"	Polished Ebony	2,900.
WLE 410	41"	Polished Mahogany	2,990.
WLE 410	41"	Polished Ivory	2,900.
WLF 430	43"	French Provincial Cherry	3,390.
WLF 430	43"	Italian Provincial Walnut	3,390.
WLF 430	43"	Mediterranean Oak	3,390.
WLF 430	43"	Queen Anne Cherry/Oak	3,390.
WLF 430	43"	Mahogany	3,390.
WLE 470	47"	Polished Ebony	3,800.
WLE 470	47"	Polished Mahogany	3,900.
WLF 470	47"	Cherry	3,580.
WLF 470	47"	Mediterranean Oak	3,580.
WLE 475	47"	Polished Mahogany	3,840.
WLE 480N	48"	Polished Ebony	3,560.
WLE 480N	48"	Polished Mahogany/Walnut/Bubinga	3,680.
WLE 510N	51"	Polished Ebony	3,770.
WLE 510N	51"	Polished Mahogany/Bubinga	3,890.

"Dynasty" Verticals

Model	Size	Style and Finish	Price*
WDE 410	41"	Polished Ebony	3,590.
WDE 410	41"	Polished Mahogany	3,700.
WDE 410	41"	Polished Ivory	3,590.
WDF 440	44"	French Provincial Cherry	3,990.
WDF 440	44"	Mediterranean Oak	3,990.
WDF 440	44"	Queen Anne Cherry/Oak	3,990.
WDE 460S	46"	Polished Ebony	4,350.
WDE 460S	46"	Polished Mahogany	4,500.
WDE 470	47"	Polished Mahogany	4,520.
WDE 480S	48"	Polished Ebony	4,390.
WDE 480S	48"	Polished Mahogany	4,520.
WDE 480S	48"	Polished Birch Burl	4,520.
WDE 510E	51"	Polished Ebony	4,790.
WDE 510E	51"	Polished Mahogany	4,990.

"Sovereign" Verticals

Model	Size	Style and Finish	Price*
WSF 44	44"	French Provincial Cherry	5,790.
WSF 44	44"	Mediterranean Oak	5,390.
WSF 44	44"	Queen Anne Cherry/Oak	5,390.
WSF 44	44"	Mahogany	5,390.

*For explanation of terms and prices, please see pages 59–65.

Weber (continued)

Model	Size	Style and Finish	Price*
WSE 46	46"	Ebony	5,390.
WSE 46	46"	American Oak/Walnut	5,590.
WSE 46	46"	Cherry	5,790.
WSF 46	46"	French Provincial Cherry	6,290.
WSF 46	46"	Mediterranean Oak	6,080.
WSF 46	46"	Mahogany	6,080.
WSE 47	47"	Ebony	5,390.
WSE 47	47"	Polished Ebony	5,190.
WSE 47	47"	Polished Mahogany/Oak	5,390.
WSE 47	47"	Walnut and Polished Walnut	5,390.
WSE 48	48"	Ebony	5,590.
WSE 48	48"	Polished Ebony	5,390.
WSE 48	48"	Mahogany/Oak/Walnut	5,790.
WSE 48	48"	Polished Mahogany/Oak/Walnut	5,590.
WSE 52	52"	Ebony	6,390.
WSE 52	52"	Polished Ebony	6,290.

"Albert Weber" Verticals

Model	Size	Style and Finish	Price*
AW 48	48"	Polished Ebony	7,990.
AW 48	48"	Birch Burl/Bubinga/Cherry/Rosewood	7,990.
AW 48	48"	Polished Mahogany	7,990.
AW 49	49"	Bubinga	8,990.
AW 49	49"	Polished Mahogany	8,990.
AW 52	52"	Polished Ebony	9,990.
AW 52	52"	Bubinga/Rosewood	9,990.

"Legend" Grands

Model	Size	Style and Finish	Price*
WLG 50S	4' 11"	Polished Ebony	8,810.
WLG 50S	4' 11"	Polished Mahogany	8,810.
WLG 50S	4' 11"	Polished Ivory	8,810.
WLG 51S	5' 2"	Polished Ebony	9,860.
WLG 51S	5' 2"	Polished Mahogany	9,980.
WLG 51S	5' 2"	Polished Ivory	9,860.
WLG 57S	5' 7"	Polished Ebony	11,120.
WLG 57S	5' 7"	Polished Mahogany	11,320.
WLG 60S	6'	Polished Ebony	11,960.
WLG 60S	6'	Polished Mahogany	12,300.

"Dynasty" Grands

Model	Size	Style and Finish	Price*
WDG 50S	4' 11"	Polished Ebony	10,390.
WDG 50S	4' 11"	Polished Mahogany	10,590.

Model	Size	Style and Finish	Price*
WDG 50S	4' 11"	Polished Walnut	10,790.
WDG 50S	4' 11"	Polished Ivory	10,390.
WDG 51S	5' 2"	Polished Ebony	11,590.
WDG 51S	5' 2"	Polished Mahogany/Walnut	11,790.
WDG 51S	5' 2"	Polished Ivory	11,790.
WDG 57S	5' 7"	Polished Ebony	12,390.
WDG 57S	5' 7"	Polished Mahogany/Walnut	12,590.
WDG 60S	6'	Polished Ebony	13,390.
WDG 60S	6'	Polished Mahogany/Walnut	13,590.

"Sovereign" Grands

Model	Size	Style and Finish	Price*
WSG 50	4' 11"	Ebony	13,790.
WSG 50	4' 11"	Polished Ebony	13,590.
WSG 50	4' 11"	Polished Mahogany	14,790.
WSG 50	4' 11"	Walnut and Polished Walnut	14,390.
WSG 50	4' 11"	Cherry	15,190.
WSG 50	4' 11"	Polished Ivory/White	13,790.
WSG 50	4' 11"	Queen Anne Polished Mahogany	15,990.
WSG 50	4' 11"	Queen Anne Cherry	16,990.
WSG 50	4' 11"	Queen Anne Polished Ivory/White	15,990.
WSG 51	5' 2"	Ebony and Polished Ebony	14,390.
WSG 51	5' 2"	Walnut	15,190.
WSG 51	5' 2"	Polished Mahogany/Walnut	14,990.
WSG 51	5' 2"	Cherry	15,590.
WSG 51	5' 2"	Oak	14,990.
WSG 51	5' 2"	Polished Ivory	14,790.
WSG 51	5' 2"	Polished White	14,590.
WSG 51	5' 2"	Queen Anne Mahogany	17,990.
WSG 51	5' 2"	Queen Anne Cherry	18,190.
WSG 51	5' 2"	Queen Anne Polished Ivory	17,590.
WSG 51	5' 2"	Country French Cherry	18,190.
WSG 57	5' 7"	Ebony	16,390.
WSG 57	5' 7"	Polished Ebony	16,190.
WSG 57	5' 7"	Walnut/Cherry	16,990.
WSG 57	5' 7"	Oak	16,790.
WSG 57	5' 7"	Polished Mahogany/Walnut	16,790.
WSG 57	5' 7"	Polished Ivory	16,590.
WSG 57	5' 7"	Country French Cherry	18,190.
WSG 60	6'	Ebony	17,990.
WSG 60	6'	Polished Ebony	17,790.
WSG 60	6'	Walnut	18,990.

*For explanation of terms and prices, please see pages 59–65.

Model	Size	Style and Finish	Price*

Weber (continued)

WSG 60	6'	Polished Mahogany/Walnut	18,790.
WSG 60	6'	Polished Ivory	19,220.

"Albert Weber" Grands

AW 51R	5' 2"	Polished Ebony	17,990.
AW 51R	5' 2"	Polished Mahogany	18,390.
AW 57R	5' 7"	Ebony and Polished Ebony	19,990.
AW 57R	5' 7"	Cherry	20,590.
AW 57R	5' 7"	Polished Mahogany/Bubinga	20,590.
AW 60R	6'	Ebony and Polished Ebony	23,390.
AW 60R	6'	Cherry	28,990.
AW 60R	6'	Polished Mahogany	23,990.
AW 60R	6'	Polished Bubinga	25,990.
AW 60R	6'	Polished Rosewood	27,990.
AW 60R	6'	Polished Pommele	28,990.
AW 69R	6' 9"	Ebony	26,390.
AW 69R	6' 9"	Polished Ebony	25,990.
AW 69R	6' 9"	Cherry	34,390.
AW 69R	6' 9"	Polished Bubinga	30,990.
AW 69R	6' 9"	Polished Rosewood	32,990.
AW 69R	6' 9"	Polished Birch Burl	33,990.
AW 69R	6' 9"	Polished Pommele	34,390.
AW 76R	7' 6"	Ebony	36,590.
AW 76R	7' 6"	Polished Ebony	36,390.
AW 76R	7' 6"	Polished Bubinga	40,590.
AW 76R	7' 6"	Polished Rosewood	41,990.
AW 76R	7' 6"	Polished Pommele	42,790.

Weinbach

Note: Prices below do not include bench. Add from $220 to $630 (most are under $400), depending on choice of bench.

Verticals

114-I	45"	Demi-Chip. Pol. Ebony/Walnut/Mahogany	6,980.
114-IC	45"	Chippendale Pol. Ebony/Walnut/Mahogany	7,180.
114-II	45"	Polished Ebony	6,100.
114-IV	45"	Polished Ebony/Walnut/Mahogany	6,580.
124-III	50"	Polished Ebony/Walnut/Mahogany	7,900.

Model	Size	Style and Finish	Price*

Grands

155	5' 3"	Polished Ebony/Walnut/Mahogany	21,000.
170	5' 8"	Polished Ebony/Walnut/Mahogany	22,200.
170	5' 8"	"Klasik" Polished Ebony/Walnut/Mahogany	25,800.
170 C	5' 8"	Chippendale Polished Walnut/Mahogany	26,500.
192	6' 4"	Polished Ebony/Walnut/Mahogany	25,600.
192	6' 4"	"Majestic" Pol. Ebony/Walnut/Mahogany	28,600.

Weinberger

Prices do not include bench.

Verticals

Friend	45"	Polished Ebony	13,111.
Friend	45"	Polished Mahogany/Dark Walnut	14,367.
Friend	45"	Walnut	13,302.
Friend	45"	Cherry	13,548.
Friend	45"	Polished Cherry	14,613.
Friend	45"	Beech/Alder	13,111.
Friend	45"	Polished White	14,776.
Vision One	47"	Polished Ebony	14,695.
Vision One	47"	Polished Mahogany/Dark Walnut	16,169.
Vision One	47"	Walnut	14,968.
Vision One	47"	Cherry	15,186.
Vision One	47"	Polished Cherry	16,333.
Vision One	47"	Beech/Alder	14,695.
Vision One	47"	Polished White	16,333.
Education	49"	Polished Ebony	8,798.

Grands

Passion	5' 7"	Polished Ebony	51,748.
Passion	5' 7"	Other Finishes (above)	on request

Wurlitzer

Grands

C143	4' 7"	Polished Ebony	9,028.
C143	4' 7"	Polished Mahogany/Oak	9,298.
C143	4' 7"	Polished White	9,028.
C153	5' 1"	Ebony and Polished Ebony	10,440.

*For explanation of terms and prices, please see pages 59–65.

Model	Size	Style and Finish	Price*

Wurlitzer (continued)

Model	Size	Style and Finish	Price*
C153	5' 1"	Polished Mahogany	10,800.
C153	5' 1"	Oak/Walnut	10,800.
C153	5' 1"	Polished Ivory	10,440.
C153QA	5' 1"	Queen Anne Polished Mahogany	12,600.
C153QA	5' 1"	Queen Anne Oak/Cherry	12,600.
C173	5' 8"	Ebony and Polished Ebony	11,520.
C173	5' 8"	Polished Mahogany	11,872.
C173	5' 8"	Polished White	11,520.

Wyman

Verticals

Model	Size	Style and Finish	Price*
WV108	42-1/2"	Continental Polished Ebony	2,790.
WV108	42-1/2"	Continental Polished Mahogany/Cherry	2,850.
WV110	43"	Polished Ebony	3,190.
WV110	43"	Polished Mahogany/Cherry	3,250.
WV110	43"	American Country Gallery Oak	3,790.
WV110	43"	Sable Brown Mahogany	3,790.
WV110	43"	French Provincial Sable Cherry	3,850.
WV110	43"	Country French Oak	3,850.
WV115	45"	Polished Ebony	3,390.
WV115	45"	Polished Mahgoany/Cherry	3,450.
WV118	46-1/2"	Polished Ebony	3,990.
WV118	46-1/2"	Cherry	4,050.
WV120	48"	Polished Ebony	3,790.
WV120	48"	Polished Mahogany	3,850.
WV132	52"	Polished Ebony	4,790.

Grands

Model	Size	Style and Finish	Price*
WG145	4' 9"	Ebony	8,190.
WG145	4' 9"	Polished Ebony	7,590.
WG145	4' 9"	Mahogany	8,190.
WG145	4' 9"	Polished Mahogany/Cherry/Snow White	8,190.
WG145	4' 9"	French Cherry and Polished Cherry	8,390.
WG160	5' 3"	Ebony	9,190.
WG160	5' 3"	Polished Ebony	8,590.
WG160	5' 3"	Mahogany and Polished Mahogany	9,190.
WG160	5' 3"	French Cherry	9,390.
WG160	5' 3"	French Polished Mahogany	9,390.

Model	Size	Style and Finish	Price*
WG170	5' 7"	Ebony	9,790.
WG170	5' 7"	Polished Ebony	9,190.
WG170	5' 7"	Mahogany and Polished Mahogany	9,790.
WG170	5' 7"	French Mahogany	9,990.
WG185	6' 1"	Polished Ebony	11,990.
WG185	6' 1"	Polished Mahogany	12,590.

Yamaha

Verticals

Model	Size	Style and Finish	Price*
M112	44"	Continental Ebony	5,090.
M112	44"	Continental Polished Ebony	5,190.
M112	44"	Continental American Walnut	5,290.
M112	44"	Continental Polished Mahogany	6,390.
M112	44"	Continental Polished Ivory/White	6,290.
M425	44"	Mahogany	3,390.
M450	44"	Cherry/Brown Cherry	3,790.
M475	44"	Mahogany	4,290.
M475	44"	Italian Provincial Dark Cherry	4,290.
M500	44"	Chippendale Brown Mahogany	5,990.
M500	44"	Florentine Light Oak	4,890.
M500	44"	Georgian Mahogany	5,990.
M500	44"	Hancock Brown Cherry	4,290.
M500	44"	Milano Dark Oak	4,890.
M500	44"	Parisian Cherry/Dark Cherry	6,190.
M500	44"	Queen Anne Cherry/Dark Cherry	5,090.
M500	44"	Sheraton Mahogany	4,290.
P22	45"	Ebony	5,190.
P22	45"	American Walnut	5,190.
P22	45"	Black, Dark, or Light Oak	5,190.
T116	45"	Ebony	3,990.
T116	45"	Polished Ebony	5,390.
T116S	45"	Polished Ebony with Silver Hardware	5,790.
T116	45"	Polished Mahogany	6,390.
P600	45"	Sheraton Brown Mahogany	5,990.
P600	45"	Queen Anne Brown Cherry	5,990.
P600	45"	Tuscan Ash	6,190.
T121	48"	Polished Ebony	6,500.
U1	48"	Ebony	8,350.
U1	48"	Polished Ebony	8,100.

*For explanation of terms and prices, please see pages 59–65.

Model	Size	Style and Finish	Price*

Yamaha (continued)

Model	Size	Style and Finish	Price*
U1	48"	American Walnut	8,900.
U1	48"	Polished American Walnut/Mahogany	9,500.
U1	48"	Polished White	9,590.
U3	52"	Polished Ebony	10,990.
U3	52"	American Walnut	11,790.
U3	52"	Polished Mahogany	12,790.
U5	52"	Polished Ebony	13,390.

Disklavier Verticals

Model	Size	Style and Finish	Price*
MX500	44"	Chippendale Brown Mahogany	11,390.
MX500	44"	Florentine Light Oak	9,790
MX500	44"	Georgian Mahogany	10,790.
MX500	44"	Milano Dark Oak	9,790
MX500	44"	Parisian Cherry and Dark Cherry	10,990.
MX500	44"	Queen Anne Cherry and Dark Cherry	9,990.
MX22	45"	American Walnut	10,190.
MX22	45"	Dark, Black, and Light Oak	10,190.
MX116	45"	Polished Ebony	10,390.
MX116	45"	Polished Mahogany	11,390
MX600	45"	Sheraton Brown Mahogany	10,990.
MX600	45"	Queen Anne Dark Cherry	10,990.
MX600	45"	Tuscan Ash	11,190.

MIDIPiano (Silent) Verticals

Model	Size	Style and Finish	Price*
MP500	44"	Cottage Cherry	7,590.
MP500	44"	Florentine Light Oak	7,590.
MP500	44"	Georgian Mahogany	8,590.
MP500	44"	Hancock Brown Cherry	7,090.
MP500	44"	Milano Dark Oak	7,590.
MP500	44"	Parisian Cherry	8,790.
MP500	44"	Queen Anne Cherry and Dark Cherry	7,790.
MP500	44"	Sheraton Mahogany	7,090.
MP22	45"	American Walnut	7,790.
MPU1	48"	Polished Ebony	10,790.

Disklavier Verticals with Silent Feature

Model	Size	Style and Finish	Price*
DU1A	48"	Polished Ebony	15,790.
DU1A	48"	American Walnut	16,390.
DU1A	48"	Polished Mahogany	17,090.
DU1A	48"	Polished White	17,190.

Model	Size	Style and Finish	Price*
Grands			
GB1	4' 11"	Polished Ebony	10,190.
GB1	4' 11"	Polished American Walnut/Mahogany	11,790.
GC1	5' 3"	Ebony	15,990.
GC1	5' 3"	Polished Ebony	15,790.
GC1	5' 3"	American Walnut	17,500.
GC1	5' 3"	Polished Mahogany/American Walnut	17,500.
GC1	5' 3"	Polished Ivory/White	17,100.
GC1FP	5' 3"	French Provincial Brown Cherry	18,590.
GC1G	5' 3"	Georgian Brown Mahogany	18,590.
C1	5' 3"	Ebony	20,790.
C1	5' 3"	Polished Ebony	20,390.
C1	5' 3"	American Walnut	23,100.
C1	5' 3"	Polished American Walnut	23,990.
C1	5' 3"	Mahogany and Polished Mahogany	23,990.
C1	5' 3"	Polished White	23,100.
C1	5' 3"	"Metro" Polished Ebony and Gold	24,590.
C2	5' 8"	Ebony	23,500.
C2	5' 8"	Polished Ebony	22,990.
C2	5' 8"	American Walnut	26,390.
C2	5' 8"	Polished American Walnut/Mahogany	27,190.
C2	5' 8"	Light American Oak	26,390.
C2	5' 8"	Polished White	24,790.
C3	6' 1"	Ebony	31,990.
C3	6' 1"	Polished Ebony	31,390.
C3	6' 1"	American Walnut	34,790.
C3	6' 1"	Polished Mahogany	36,690.
C3	6' 1"	Polished White	35,390.
S4	6' 3"	Polished Ebony	56,700.
C5	6' 7"	Ebony	34,590.
C5	6' 7"	Polished Ebony	33,990.
C5	6' 7"	Polished Mahogany	43,500.
C6	6' 11"	Ebony	38,500.
C6	6' 11"	Polished Ebony	37,900.
C6	6' 11"	Polished Mahogany	45,590.
S6	6' 11"	Polished Ebony	64,300.
C7	7' 6"	Ebony	43,900.
C7	7' 6"	Polished Ebony	43,500.
C7	7' 6"	Polished Mahogany	49,900.

*For explanation of terms and prices, please see pages 59–65.

Yamaha (continued)

Model	Size	Style and Finish	Price*
CFIIIS	9'	Ebony	117,390.
CFIIIS	9'	Polished Ebony	115,990.

Disklavier Grands

Model	Size	Style and Finish	Price*
DGB1	4' 11"	Polished Ebony (playback only)	17,590.
DGB1	4' 11"	Polished Mahogany/Walnut (playback only)	19,190.
DGC1	5' 3"	Polished Ebony (playback only)	23,390.
DGC1M4	5' 3"	Ebony	32,190.
DGC1M4	5' 3"	Polished Ebony	31,990.
DGC1M4	5' 3"	American Walnut	33,590.
DGC1M4	5' 3"	Polished American Walnut/Mahogany	33,590.
DGC1M4	5' 3"	Polished Ivory/White	33,190.
DC1M4	5' 3"	Ebony	37,790.
DC1M4	5' 3"	Polished Ebony	37,590.
DC1M4	5' 3"	American Walnut	39,990.
DC1M4	5' 3"	Polished American Walnut	40,990.
DC1M4	5' 3"	Mahogany and Polished Mahogany	40,990.
DC1M4	5' 3"	Polished White	39,990.
DC2M4	5' 8"	Ebony	40,190.
DC2M4	5' 8"	Polished Ebony	39,990.
DC2M4	5' 8"	American Walnut	42,990.
DC2M4	5' 8"	Polished American Walnut/Mahogany	43,790.
DC2M4	5' 8"	Polished Light American Oak	42,990.
DC2M4	5' 8"	Polished White	41,790.
DC3M4t	6' 1"	Ebony	51,390.
DC3M4t	6' 1"	Polished Ebony	50,990.
DC3M4t	6' 1"	American Walnut	53,990.
DC3M4t	6' 1"	Polished Mahogany	55,790.
DC3M4t	6' 1"	Polished White	54,590.
DC5M4t	6' 7"	Ebony	59,390.
DC5M4t	6' 7"	Polished Ebony	58,990.
DC5M4t	6' 7"	Polished Mahogany	67,990.
DC6M4t	6' 11"	Ebony	66,590.
DC6M4t	6' 11"	Polished Ebony	65,990.
DC6M4t	6' 11"	Polished Mahogany	73,990.
DC7M4t	7' 6"	Ebony	74,390.
DC7M4t	7' 6"	Polished Ebony	73,990.

Model	Size	Style and Finish	Price*

Disklavier Pro Grands

Model	Size	Style and Finish	Price*
DC3M4PRO	6' 1"	Polished Ebony	55,990.
DS4M4PRO	6' 3"	Polished Ebony	77,990.
DC5M4PRO	6' 7"	Polished Ebony	61,990.
DC6M4PRO	6' 11"	Polished Ebony	67,990.
DS6M4PRO	6' 11"	Polished Ebony	83,990.
DC7M4PRO	7' 6"	Polished Ebony	73,990.
DCFIIISM4PRO	9'	Polished Ebony	149,990.

MIDIPiano (Silent) Grands

Model	Size	Style and Finish	Price*
MPC1	5' 3"	Polished Ebony	25,190.
MPC2	5' 8"	Polished Ebony	27,790.
MPC3	6' 1"	Polished Ebony	35,890.
MPC6	6' 11"	Polished Ebony	41,990.
MPC7	7' 6"	Polished Ebony	47,290.

Young Chang

See also under "Bergmann" and "Weber."

Verticals

Model	Size	Style and Finish	Price*
GE-102	43"	Continental Polished Ebony	3,590.
GE-102	43"	Continental Polished Mahogany	3,700.
GE-102	43"	Continental Polished Ivory	3,590.
GF-110	43-1/2"	Queen Anne Oak/Cherry	3,990.
GF-110	43-1/2"	Mediterranean Oak	3,990.
GF-110	43-1/2"	French Provincial Cherry	3,990.
PF-110	43-1/2"	Mahogany	5,390.
PF-110	43-1/2"	Queen Anne Oak/Cherry	5,390.
PF-110	43-1/2"	Mediterranean Oak	5,390.
PF-110	43-1/2"	French Provincial Cherry	5,790.
GE-116	46-1/2"	Polished Ebony	4,350.
GE-116	46-1/2"	Polished Mahogany	4,500.
PF-116	46-1/2"	Mahogany	6,080.
PF-116	46-1/2"	Mediterranean Oak	6,080.
PF-116	46-1/2"	French Provincial Cherry	6,290.
PE-116S	46-1/2"	Ebony	5,390.
PE-116S	46-1/2"	American Walnut/Oak	5,590.
PE-116S	46-1/2"	American Cherry	5,790.
PE-118	47"	Ebony	5,390.
PE-118	47"	Polished Ebony	5,190.

*For explanation of terms and prices, please see pages 59–65.

Model	Size	Style and Finish	Price*

Young Chang (continued)

Model	Size	Style and Finish	Price*
PE-118	47"	Polished Mahogany/Walnut/Oak	5,390.
PE-118	47"	Walnut	5,390.
GE-121	48"	Polished Ebony	4,390.
GE-121	48"	Polished Mahogany	4,520.
GE-121	48"	Polished Birch Burl	4,520.
PE-121	48"	Ebony	5,590.
PE-121	48"	Polished Ebony	5,390.
PE-121	48"	Mahogany/Walnut/Oak	5,790.
PE-121	48"	Polished Mahogany/Walnut/Oak	5,590.
YP 48	48"	Polished Ebony	7,990.
YP 48	48"	Mahogany/Cherry/Bubinga/Rosewood	7,990.
YP 49	49"	Mahogany/Bubinga	8,990.
GE-131	52"	Polished Ebony	4,790.
GE-131	52"	Polished Mahogany	4,990.
PE-131	52"	Ebony	6,390.
PE-131	52"	Polished Ebony	6,290.
YP 52	52"	Polished Ebony	9,990.
YP 52	52"	Bubinga/Rosewood	9,990.

Grands

Model	Size	Style and Finish	Price*
GS-150	4' 11-1/2"	Polished Ebony	10,390.
GS-150	4' 11-1/2"	Polished Mahogany	10,590.
GS-150	4' 11-1/2"	Polished Walnut	10,790.
GS-150	4' 11-1/2"	Polished Ivory	10,390.
PG-150	4' 11-1/2"	Ebony	13,790.
PG-150	4' 11-1/2"	Polished Ebony	13,590.
PG-150	4' 11-1/2"	Polished Mahogany	14,790.
PG-150	4' 11-1/2"	Walnut and Polished Walnut	14,390.
PG-150	4' 11-1/2"	Cherry	15,190.
PG-150	4' 11-1/2"	Polished Ivory/White	13,790.
PG-150	4' 11-1/2"	Queen Anne Polished Mahogany	15,990.
PG-150	4' 11-1/2"	Queen Anne Cherry	16,990.
PG-150	4' 11-1/2"	Queen Anne Polished Ivory/White	15,990.
GS-157	5' 2"	Polished Ebony	11,590.
GS-157	5' 2"	Polished Mahogany/Walnut	11,790.
GS-157	5' 2"	Polished Ivory	11,790.
PG-157	5' 2"	Ebony and Polished Ebony	14,390.
PG-157	5' 2"	Polished Mahogany	14,990.
PG-157	5' 2"	Walnut	15,190.
PG-157	5' 2"	Polished Walnut	14,990.

Model	Size	Style and Finish	Price*
PG-157	5' 2"	Cherry	15,590.
PG-157	5' 2"	Oak	14,990.
PG-157	5' 2"	Polished Ivory	14,790.
PG-157	5' 2"	Polished White	14,590.
PG-157	5' 2"	Country French Cherry	18,190.
PG-157	5' 2"	Queen Anne Mahogany	17,990.
PG-157	5' 2"	Queen Anne Cherry	18,190.
PG-157	5' 2"	Queen Anne Polished Ivory	17,590.
PG-157	5' 2"	Empire Polished Mahogany	17,790.
YP 157	5' 2"	Polished Ebony	17,990.
YP 157	5' 2"	Polished Mahogany	18,390.
GS-175	5' 9"	Polished Ebony	12,390.
GS-175	5' 9"	Polished Mahogany/Walnut	12,590.
PG-175	5' 9"	Ebony	16,390.
PG-175	5' 9"	Polished Ebony	16,190.
PG-175	5' 9"	Polished Mahogany	16,790.
PG-175	5' 9"	Walnut	16,990.
PG-175	5' 9"	Polished Walnut	16,790.
PG-175	5' 9"	Cherry	16,390.
PG-175	5' 9"	Oak	16,790.
PG-175	5' 9"	Polished Ivory	16,590.
PG-175	5' 9"	Country French Cherry	18,190.
PG-175	5' 9"	Empire Polished Mahogany	18,790.
YP 175	5' 9"	Ebony and Polished Ebony	19,990.
YP 175	5' 9"	Cherry	20,590.
YP 175	5' 9"	Polished Mahogany/Bubinga	20,590.
PG-185	6' 1"	Ebony	17,990.
PG-185	6' 1"	Polished Ebony	17,790.
PG-185	6' 1"	Walnut	18,990.
PG-185	6' 1"	Polished Mahogany/Walnut	18,790.
PG-185	6' 1"	Polished Ivory	19,220.
YP 185	6' 1"	Ebony and Polished Ebony	23,390.
YP 185	6' 1"	Cherry	28,990.
YP 185	6' 1"	Polished Mahogany	23,990.
YP 185	6' 1"	Polished Bubinga	25,990.
YP 185	6' 1"	Polished Rosewood	27,990.
YP 185	6' 1"	Polished Pommele	28,990.
YP 185C	6' 1"	Polished Mahogany	25,790.
PG-208	6' 10"	Ebony	24,790.
PG-208	6' 10"	Polished Ebony	23,090.
PG-208	6' 10"	Oak	27,990.

*For explanation of terms and prices, please see pages 59–65.

Model	Size	Style and Finish	Price*

Young Chang (continued)

Model	Size	Style and Finish	Price*
PG-208	6' 10"	Polished White	24,990.
YP 208R	6' 10"	Ebony	26,390.
YP 208R	6' 10"	Polished Ebony	25,990.
YP 208R	6' 10"	Cherry	34,390.
YP 208R	6' 10"	Polished Bubinga	30,990.
YP 208R	6' 10"	Polished Rosewood	32,990.
YP 208R	6' 10"	Polished Birch Burl	33,990.
YP 208R	6' 10"	Polished Pommele	34,390.
PG-213	7'	Ebony	28,190.
PG-213	7'	Polished Ebony	27,990.
YP 228R	7' 6"	Ebony	36,590.
YP 228R	7' 6"	Polished Ebony	36,390.
YP 228R	7' 6"	Polished Bubinga	40,590.
YP 228R	7' 6"	Polished Rosewood	41,990.
YP 228R	7' 6"	Polished Pommele	42,790.